THE LISNAGOOLA CHRONICLES

Brendan Hoban

The Lisnagoola Chronicles
MUSINGS ON THE CLERICAL LIFE

the columba press

First edition published in 1995 by
τhe columba press
93 The Rise, Mount Merrion, Blackrock, Co Dublin, Ireland

Cover by Bill Bolger
Origination by The Columba Press
Printed in Ireland by Genprint Ltd, Dublin

ISBN 1 85607 134 0

Acknowledgements

My thanks to Cyprian Candon O.P., former editor of *Intercom*,
who originally prompted me to develop the *Pastor Rusticus* per-
sona and my subsequent musings in the pages of *Intercom*; and
to editors, Tom O'Loughlin and Kevin Hegarty, and their staff,
for facilitating that indulgence.

Contents

Dedication
To the late Monsignor Tommy Waldron

I The first word

I require, as the redoubtable Anthony Burgess would have put it, a sententious opening, some affectedly formal *entrée* on to the Lisnagoola stage. After a long and definitively tedious career in one of the least impressive vineyards of the Lord, I have been persuaded, *admirabile dictu*, to share my musings on this priestly life with a wider audience. Having for some years addressed occasional epistles to my devoted readers in the august columns of *Intercom* and at the same time prised appropriately gargantuan stipends from their Lordships' purses *à la* The Catholic Communications Institute of Ireland, I was assured that throngs, indeed veritable hosts, of readers have become addicted to my beguiling mixture of personal abuse and self-deprecation. Hence the effort to capitalise on their exceedingly good taste, as Mr Kipling would say, and I anticipate, with salivating delight, the responsible disposal of whatever royalties may subsequently emerge for the worthiest of good causes. No, not the Third World or youth employment or some such aspiration to which so many of us rhapsodically allocate vast sums from the proceeds of an imminent Lotto win. Nor indeed would I direct it towards financing that most indispensible of liturgical artefacts, an inside toilet in the sacristy. Rather, a long sabbatical in Provence is planned, where I hope to patronise the natives, do some research into local wines and learn to play the bagpipes, a foible to which, as my few friends will attest, I am somewhat excessively addicted.

I should, of course, at the outset, summon a suitably pretentious couplet from some obscure modern poet not just to declaim the earth-shattering news that the pastor of St Bridget's, Lisnagoola has decided to reveal something less than all, but also to declaim the absurdly literate (not to say erudite) tone I will attempt to sustain in these musings. There are those who, because of incredibly poor taste or the onset of senescense or some peculiar angst that congenitally afflicts the ecclesiastical psyche, may dismiss my style as affected, pretentious, declamatory, even foppish and this tome a literary doily to titivate stylistic pretensions. I know what such fiends are at, if you'll pardon the grammatical construction. In a word, or rather two, *invidia clericalis*. One (the anglicised impersonal singular seems somehow appropriate) is, like Prince Charles, always conscious that clerical life and even one's own confrères have an unenviable tendency to dampen one's expectations. Indeed in his definitive study, *The Priest of Today; His Ideals and His Duties*, published as recently as 1909, The Reverend and revered Thomas O'Donnell relates that 'in the clerical as in every other human heart there are passions that struggle against the reign of charity'. Who are you telling, Tom, who are you telling? 'An envious splenetic disposition', he goes on, should make way for 'a habit of sympathetic appreciation' which, even allowing for the elegant language of his time, 'will make our intercourse with others sweet and harmonious'. Indeed.

But first I should enter a string of caveats. In my former epistles – if you'll pardon the side-step into Jane Austen country – I have often stood accused – taken to task, wings clipped, halt to my gallop, wind out of my sails, sort of thing – not for murdering the English language for which a considerable book of evidence could be compiled; nor for some antisocial idiosyncrasy endemic to a life of celibacy (for which ... well, let's not get into that, just yet); nor for the natural ease with which I have embraced that most endeavouring of personal philosophies, *festina lente*; or even for expecting readers to cope with impossibly long sentences.

No, what was usually at issue was some presumed allusion to a colleague in passing. He would then upbraid me for my effrontery not to say insolence in, as one delightfully put it, 'exposing him to the entire country', an unhappy phrase in an age ruthlessly dedicated to a relentless search not for meaning but for

double entendre. Another colleague imagined himself to be the
mythical curate to whom, I had apparently alleged, a video-
recorder had been presented in depressing circumstances in a
previous dispensation. In chronicling the ordinary and uneventful, there is the danger of some clerical Narcissus imagining
himself playing the main part on every stage, real or imagined.
The great difficulty with the clerical life is that most of us have
ordinariness, if not idleness, thrust upon us. We are not, most of
us, remarkable people and those of us who think we are haven't
lived long enough to discover we're not.

There is a point to be made and it obviously bears repetition. In a
largely fictitious work such as this, a certain distortion is clearly
in order, a prosaic licence if you will, if not to foment a flame of
excitement at least to keep some flicker of interest alive. The
truth, as Burgess would have it, is a moveable feast, a variable
commodity, fabled by the sons and daughters of memory. The
irrepressible Fr Derek, for example, is not modelled on any particular individual. (Is there, I ask rhetorically, in the length and
breadth of this green and already troubled land, a Fr Derek?
And the voices reply, 'Yes, a host beyond compare!') He is rather
an amalgam of hopefully identifiable features in Irish clerical
life, a hybrid who, for your distraction and my own merriment,
is personified in the swish curate in Lisnagoola. There is, I consider, something to be said for presenting 'a type' of the unremarkable and embellishing it with a medley of experience and
invention, the remembered and the imagined. At the same time I
have no illusions about becoming a latterday Francis Thompson
parking his chariot somewhere between Heaven and Charing
Cross or, in my case, between the heathery slopes of Slieve
Gowna and the rude Atlantic.

So when I set in some relief the inevitable disparity between aspiration and achievement in Irish Church life, when I record the
endearing and sometimes even bizarre eccentricities of my confrères, when I relate the fables of Lisnagoola, you (dear reader)
are not the hero of every story. All of you is not in any of these
chronicles (if you'll pardon the grammar) but some part of you
may feature in quite a few. 'I am all the daughters of my father's

house,' said the intrepid heroine in *Twelfth Night*, 'and all the brothers too'.

A further caveat. The appalling prospect of actually conspiring to set myself the kind of deadlines that will, over a modest period, produce thousands of words is normally a consummation to be devoutly avoided. So something by way of antecedent *apologia* is in order. This task is not undertaken in the belief that the thoughts I convey, or the florid and occasionally purple prose I misuse to convey them, will edify or instruct those sufficiently gifted by God to read them. No, I write, as I suspect most people write, for private enjoyment and, once bitten, nothing quite inoculates against the bug that beckons towards a blank sheet of paper. Writing is a lonely and solitary task but it is done not just because it is, in Flaubert's phrase, 'adventuring with language' but because, as William Faulkner once said, 'it's worth the trouble'. There is the other consideration that writing is the least complicated of the three great compulsions that surface as the years trundle past: planting a tree, parenting a child, writing a book. While a tree had to die somewhere to give me the luxury of these pages, my reluctance to expend any more energy than suffices to keep my pipe alight dissuades me from revisiting that foreign land called The Dignity of Labour. 'Work', as Bertrand Russell once observed, 'is of two kinds. The first involves altering the position of matter relative to the earth's surface; the second consists in telling people to do so.' I am, as experience has taught me, more at home in the second camp. Again, while the logic of our changing times, embellished with the tabloid truth, suggests that it's only a matter of time until every confrère manages to produce some offspring, I prefer to hold with the logic of the democratisation of literary culture and the burgeoning of print technology in that sooner or later everyone will eventually write a book.

A further caveat is to the effect that what I write is not just indulging some pet enthusiasm or a muddled form of literary narcissism. Having lived for more years than I care to remember the peculiarly idiosyncratic life of a rural pastor, I am for my own psychical equilibrium smitten with a certain involved bemusement at the vagaries of clerical life. Tolstoy believed that the wrongs of the world could be righted by not eating meat and learning to make your own shoes. Gandhi believed in a spare diet and weaving his own loincloths; and while I would with my customary modesty disincline any personal comparison with such revered gentlemen, I would offer my own tuppenceworth of wisdom distilled from a long and frustratingly enjoyable clerical life: the need for those who deal with the brokenness of the human condition, and the faith that gives substance to what appears to be folly, to develop a healthy regard for the human foibles through which they are so often sustained.

There is a definition of humour – which I have incidentally culled from the humourless Malcolm Muggeridge – that sees its function as expressing in terms of the grotesque the immense disparity between human aspiration and human performance. The clerical life is, as we all know, no stranger to that disparity. It is a rich vein in which to mine the sense of fun that helps to sustain the definitive seriousness of our lives. After all, Aquinas has suggested that God made the world in a spirit of play, and laughter, we're told, is the sunshine of the soul. We may not exude a sense of Easter joy in all circumstances, but God help us if a sense of humour isn't evident in some. Indeed if, in my declining years, as a result of some improbable outburst of missionary fervour I find myself marooned on a desert island, I fervently pray that, with whatever occupant I am destined to share that questionable or, after a lifetime of celibacy, possibly enviable fate, whatever qualifications for humanity he or preferably she may enjoy, a sense of humour may be one of them. Who was it said that God gives us imagination to compensate for what we are not and a sense of humour to console us for what we are? May God in his wisdom preserve us from a diet of unrelieved seriousness.

I make the point simply to indicate that to accept the reality of one's individual performance, à la Muggeridge's definition, is not to reject the general aspiration. Faith without good works may not bring us very far, as Saint James warns us, but I sometimes wonder how far we'll get with faith without good humour. Joylessness is in real danger of outstripping predictability as the great clerical sin of our time.

Yet another admission is in order. From time to time, the limited
agenda of clerical life in my particular bailiwick receives a considerable fillip with the arrival of a new bishop from, as is now
customary, a distant kingdom. New kings bring new rules, and
a new bishop, like any new pastor, brings his own style. In the
process, a certain clerical *glasnost*, if not *perestroika*, is in order.
Staid and settled conventions can find themselves hovering pre-
cariously over real or imagined chasms. The unrelieved predictability of diocesan life, sedated by decades of routine, gives
way to a gloriously disturbing uncertainty about every episcopal
attitude.

There is a certain comic, possibly anarchic, delight to be gleaned
from the sight of stolid clerics, unusually prone to taciturnity,
like skiers on a landslide giving masterly impressions of a world
disintegrating under their feet. The infinitude of life's varied
possibilities is suddenly and devastatingly appreciated alike by
thrusting young curates discomfortingly overtaken by the logic
of their own theories, middle-aged 'waiters' wavering on the
brink of achieving life's great clerical ambition, and affectedly
crabby PPs palpitating on the verge of retirement. The chronicling of such, shall we say, creative tension is a delight too lus-
cious to pass.

The space we stand in, to paraphrase Seamus Heaney, has been
emptied into us to keep. The clerical patchworks we now form
will, in future years, be left dishevelled by the pitch and toss of
history. Memory recollected not so much in tranquillity but with
a little humour and hopefully a little grace ... *momentum aere
perennius*? Or something like that.

II Mapping the territory

Lisnagoola could be Patrick Kavanagh country if Erato, that elusive offspring of Zeus, were to visit. But no Muse being – at least for some – good news, it's just another rural parish nestling between the mountains and the sea. A pleasant enough vineyard for the labourer, though lonely in an almost secretive way, damp and desolate too as winter mists steal up from the shore and camp along the hillside. A farming and, to a lesser extent, fishing people coax a sparse enough living from the inhospitable countryside and the unpredictable ocean, their lives shaped by nature's contours of sea and land, mirror images of the changing seasons, a people hearing with Wordsworth 'The still, sad music of humanity' but knowing too, with Kennelly, that

It is not a music that will live alone
Or be acquired
For good by any man.

The *Status Animarum*, inherited from a more judicious predecessor, reminds me, as it does my curate, that in less than three hundred homes there are fewer than one thousand souls, entrusted *per Deum et episcopum* to our uneven care. I propose, *Deus volens*, to share fragmentary thoughts, menopausal musings on this quiet rural drama with a cast of hundreds, a *Waiting for Godot* on a larger and possibly even more depressing stage. So I pray that the reader will pardon the infrequent solecism, and the flights of fancy that every pastor is tempted to confer numinously on his flock, not to speak of the occasional failure to resist the clerical temptation to see the lives of our people as refracted through our own, often appropriated rather than celebrated. There is, too, the truth that an everyday occurrence given a bit of prominence has a habit of being transformed into an event of some significance. A touch of Kavanagh maybe, but hopefully not Hans Christian Andersen.

Perhaps the draughts coursing through the parish church of St Brigid will temper my more whimsical delusions. St Brigid's nestles comfortably under the shadow of Slieve Gowna, giving a good impression of a stilted picture-postcard scene from an English midland village. Around the church, the fuchsia growth, cropped severely into something approaching a hedge in late Autumn, has fought back, maturing buds drooping languidly to form the unseasonal *deoríní Dé*. Inside at morning Mass the pall is requisite, rather than rubrical, in the amber light and sultry atmosphere that tempts the occasional maverick representative of the fly kingdom to hover drowsily over the chalice. Elsewhere in the church there is the uneven ululation of a captive bee as it combs the variegated windows for an avenue of escape and the murmured responses of the morning faithful, my congregation of two, Mary Sexton and Sally Preston, Mary in the south transept, Sally two seats from the back. I raise one large and two small breads on the offertory paten, silent symbols of a lonely eucharist.

It's easy to linger in St Brigid's in the morning light, to savour the atmosphere of silence, to resist the recurrent temptation to be deflected by the cares of the coming day. On the walls are the traditional Stations of the Cross, gaudy reminders of a declining devotion and a decrepit art. R. S. Thomas, in his poem, *The Minister*, equates Protestantism with 'adroit castration of art and song and dance. You have botched our flesh and left us only the soul's terrible impotence in a warm world.' Looking around St Brigid's, there is little evidence that Catholicism has kept the faith. Here before my eyes is evidence of the Anthony Burgess thesis that the philistine Catholicism of the 1930s, pursued by the Maynooth priests, drove many away from the faith. Not so, in Lisnagoola. No need here for the existence of God to be adumbrated in a beauty that pointed beyond its own delight. Our theology is considerably less aesthetic. There is no Harry Clarke or Evie Hone to give a sense that mere humans could share in the divine creativity; no Seamus Murphy to breathe life into the surrounding stone, no Ray Carroll to search out the face of God in a warming tapestry. Here we make do with the plastic indecency of electronic votive lights, a Madonna in an outrageous hue of blue, and St Joseph's epicene figure silhouetted against the back window.

And, of course, the marble plaques bearing tributes not just to priests of the past but to our unerring propensity for copying the worst excesses of Protestant iconography. One with a florid, arabesque surround, decorative to an almost vulgar degree, bears the inscription: 'To Father Michael Kelly PP of Lisnagoola 1874-1895. Died 9th February 1895. Aged 50 years. Erected by his devoted parishioners.' For what great talent or virtue or perhaps expedience I wonder was this man raised to the eminence of *Parochus* at the exceptional age of 29, the oil of ordination scarcely dry on his hands? And for what great service to humanity or saintliness did his flock mourn his passing? All that and heaven too?

Lower, appropriately, on the wall is a more modest inscription: 'Pray for the soul of Patrick Munnelly. Parish priest of this parish 1895-1908. Erected by his niece Mary Schwartz, Scranton, USA.' No devoted parishioners here to mourn the passing of a beloved pastor, no suggestion of great virtue or even modest respect but nonetheless the love of possibly a sister's child in another hemisphere. *Sic transit gloria mundi.*

My favourite inscription is hidden away under the gallery: 'In Memory of John Murphy PP. Erected by his curate, Patrick Duffy, March 1864.' The ultimate surely in approbation, an ecclesiastical Victoria Cross and Nobel Prize rolled into one, an improbable clerical tribute even in more tranquil Tridentine days. But I wander.

Can it not be said that without some sense of beauty, some feel for 'the finer things in life' there can ultimately be no faith, no God worth the effort? Or can that beauty, that goodness, that truth find its ultimate spiritual elegance in the patterns left behind by a receding tide or an expanse of Artic snow or a starry symphony in a clear sky? Or are such concerns simply too esoteric for the good people of Lisnagoola?

Sometimes their compulsions bother my soul. Like the Saturday night dance, or more recently disco, a strange amalgam of darkness and noise that provides a particularly incommunicative backdrop for the meeting of the sexes, a modern *Ballroom of Romance* in harsher, less personal colours. Or that transcultural constant of the modern Church, the weekly bingo session in the parish hall. While the excesses and repercussions of the former may be more obvious, perhaps the latter wreaks more fundamental and permanent havoc. Bingo, I assure myself, provides a harmless social outing for a group, in the main elderly and female, who after all have no alternative pastime. And there is always the question of the parish or some other debt which, like the poor, will always be with us. But on occasion between calls for two fat ladies (88) and two little ducks (22), I ponder on the distinct possibility that I may be making a significant contribution to the abolition of that cultivation of intellect and spirit, that communal and individual awareness, that richness of life, sensibility, heritage or whatever that we call 'culture.'

It is, of course, a wholly debased word because it smacks of intellectual elitism, of silly self-improvement courses, of some scruffy poet reading eminently forgettable lines to a few local eccentrics with literary pretensions in some drafty parish hall. But behind the word is a reality that gives a depth, a richness, an authenticity to life lived in place and time.

It has to do with the essential sanctity of the individual life, with prising open vistas of experience and avenues of growth that release the human spirit and give expression to a variety of loyalties and devotions that antedate the more contrived allegiances of the present day. In essence, lifting minds and hearts to an appreciation of the beauty of life and the goodness and love of God. In effect, what bingo is not.

I do not, of course, suggest that without this obtuse pastime – to which despite its ineffable tedium so many of my flock remain addicted – the literati of Lisnagoola would suddenly organise *avant garde* or esoteric literary and cultural pursuits, a Lisnagoola Arts Festival perhaps, that would contrive to function without the vocal limitations of a Mick Flavin or a Declan Nerney. Or that the local ICA would overnight develop an enthusiasm for the singing of sixteenth-century madrigals. Or local farmers bringing the milk to the creamery in Carrowhubbock would while away the time whistling arias from Verdi's operas. But it would be reasonable to presume that we would not at least set out mischievously to undermine those traditions of Irish life that we would broadly describe as 'cultural.'

On one, in retospect, notorious occasion when I shared some such reformist proposals with the members of the bingo committee, my contribution was greeted with devastating silence. I could practically hear them later on dismiss my concern as yet another unintelligible clerical foible, the kind of eccentricity that isolation or celibacy or whatever contrived to produce. That devastating rural judgement – 'He's not like the last man' – was written all over their faces. Any suggestion that bingo might be so intellectually undemanding as to be positively debilitating, even of doubtful social intercourse, questionable moral rectitude or plain silly, would be quite beyond them.

The nearest Lisnagoola gets to loftier pursuits is that narrow vision of Irish cultural life to which the GAA at least officially defers. The annual *Scór* competitions and a smattering of Irish on public occasions bear witness to a sense that there may be more to life than kicking a ball around a field.

In fact, there is in humble Lisnagoola a species of Irish kind that has, out of a coalescing of religious, political and sporting perspectives, established an identity that gives purpose and understanding to life lived in this place. I refer to what, for my own delectation, I have called the *Cagaff*, that easy alliance of Catholic/ GAA/ Fianna Fáil. Cagaffs are usually of a conservative disposition, loyalty to traditional allegiances their strong point. Religious ecumenism is tolerated, not because of any unambiguous quotation from John's gospel, but as a kind of public recognition of good community relations. Sporting ecumenism, though, is out of the question and phrases like 'other codes' and 'foreign games' help avoid any undue familiarity that might compromise the athletic purity of 'the Gael'. And the Cagaff character is fleshed out with a remorseless devotion to the 'old party' and 'core values' that would never admit to 'alien influences' like 'socialism' or whatever.

Cagaffs one and all are the backbone of my parish They join the Pioneers, take up the collections, assemble the Crib and effect a myriad of other parochial duties for the execution of which I myself over the years have developed a somewhat restrained proclivity. And of course, they organise the parish bingo on cold Winter nights as I stand in thermals and Crombie, hopping from one leg to the other, considering my contentious, and possibly pretentious, reservations about this peculiar communal addiction. And the words of Helder Camara come to mind:

Teach your child from infancy
to love open spaces.
Widen his mind.
He will be glad of this
especially if later
he must endure
a life confined
by a slit window's littleness
to one small patch of sky.

I thought of those words too when, as the consistently and unanimously retained Chairman of the local GAA club, I had to call an emergency meeting. Our under-12 football team had no sooner won the county title than it emerged that the captain was over-age. This exciting news broke some time after the victory celebrations during which I had made several speeches congratulating the local club, commending the officers for their foresight and commitment and, eventually, spending some time scraping egg off a fairly red clerical face. At the meeting I proposed that the divisional title should be handed back. I felt, wrongly as it turned out, that this gesture might help us to salvage some semblance of dignity, particularly in view of the discomforting fact that we had been forcibly relieved of the county title. The proposal was defeated on the grounds that while they understood my attitude ('You'd be expected to say that, Father'), the distilled wisdom of hundreds of GAA meetings indicated that what you have you hold ('They'd laugh at us if we gave in the cup without having to'). And anyway 'It would be letting the lads down'.

The perpetrators of the injustice were some of the most decent and honourable people in the parish. But while they listened respectfully to my sermonettes on fair play, good example and so on, it was clear that they regarded my intervention, though well-meaning, as quite irrelevant and even possibly absurd. Nice chat about justice and fair play had as little to do with GAA matters as it had with other issues like dole, grants, paying tax and so on, the real world of living and partly living.

Which experiences identified an important truth. For my good people of Lisnagoola, religion is essentially a private concern. It shouldn't be allowed impinge too much on business, social or political affairs. Its wisdom confuses, upsets, divides unless it is safely contained within its own innocuous domain, quite outside the mainstream of life. It is, I often feel, a gelded version of Christianity. Its world is that of lighted candles, organ music, the whiff of incense, social conformity. Its language that of arcane phrases so endlessly repeated as to be practically devoid of meaning. Its gestures honed by repetition to a comfortable nicety. Its moving force ritual and duty rather than the freedom of the children of God. How to bring Christ to the football field as well as on the altar; how to lift hearts and minds above and beyond the two fat ladies and the two little ducks?

And I find myself here in Lisnagoola, a restless spectator on the sideline, like a perennial substitute anxious to be involved, but somehow always apart from the real action, the pressing concerns of my people. A bit like Henri Nouwen's wounded healer, liked by a few crew members on the ship of life but not taken very seriously when the weather is fine ... *et confortetur cor tuum, et sustine Dominum.*

III God's own people

Most of us walk the pilgrim way somewhere between the faith-extremities in Heaney's *In Illo Tempore* when belief is complete and self-assured and everything reflects the presence of God:

> Altar stone was dawn and monstrance noon,
> the word rubric itself a blood-shot sunset

and an almost compulsive incredulity when

> even the range wall of the promenade
> that I press down on for conviction
> hardly tempts me to credit it.

The temptation is to run the film back. The influences and experiences of childhood form a deep well to which we tread for solace. The insoluble complexities of adult life predispose us to attempt sporadic visits to that simpler and retrospectively saintlier age. But it won't do. The great patchwork quilt of faith comes in a thousand colours.

On a Sunday morning I survey God's people in this corner of his vineyard. The same faces in the same places, as Sunday follows Sunday. For many of them this is the only world they know and they live in it without faith-anxiety among the landmarks of their own lives. The circle of birth, growth, life and death is mirrored in the seasons of their lives. There is no other truth and they search out the traces and sounds of God in the crannies of this place. As I mark the missal before Mass, fingering the silky ribbons splayed out beyond the edges, I see that Martin Murphy has arrived. The bicycle is in the shed behind the sacristy; the 'clips' in the pocket of his huge overcoat; he is kneeling on the white handkerchief he has spread on the kneeler of the last seat of the Church; and he is telling his beads. The same place, the same time, the same ritual every Sunday.

And so they gather. Sally Preston is there too, but then she is there every morning, part of that loyal remnant scrupulously faithful to daily Mass. Her morning ritual has been honed to a predictable and undeviating pattern. She opens the church, covers her head with Pauline fervour, lights the altar candles, prepares the wine and water, drapes the amice at an agreeable distance from the single-bar heater in the sacristy to counteract the possibility that any suggestion of dampness on the nape of the celebrant's neck might render him indisposed. And in deference to the consistent absence of altar-boys, rings the Mass bell from her seat. During Mass, though invariably assuming the proper postures at appropriate times, she reads her own prayers from a black prayerbook breaking at the spine from a superfluity of memorial cards and leaflet devotions to a dizzy variety of saints, authentic, prospective and relegated. After Mass she performs the Stations of the Cross, lights complicated arrangements of shrine candles and votive lights and prays before every statue in the church.

In her innocent way, high levels of clerical sanctity are taken for granted on the false assumption that contact with holy things induces holiness by osmosis. Every clerical opinion receives such unrestrained affirmation that she could on occasion easily be mistaken for the nodding icon of Berganzi. Sally is the clerical equivalent of the latter-day 'groupie', the devoted female fan who hangs around the edges of male pop stars. She is the unofficial secretary of 'Father's' fan-club. She would variously describe him as 'a nice man', 'a lovely priest', 'a saint'. No task is too menial to lessen the strain under which he is presumed to labour, no opportunity is lost to remind him of how busy he is; no detail of his uneventful life too unexciting to be endlessly remembered and repeated; no sock so worn as not to be lovingly darned to its original pristine condition; no opportunity too fleeting to avoid assuring him of how wonderful he is. Sally combines at once such an irrepressible benignity of nature and such a fascination for the minutiae of clerical life that she presents as the Irish

Catholic equivalent of Barbara Pym's 'Fine Women', the pious ladies who tend their begonias, ply the rector with gooseberry jam, and fantasise about the curate.

Jack Munnelly is there too, in the front seat. A less benign species than Maggie, he would nonetheless share her faith constituency. The thick Sunday Missal, which he studiously carries with him, bears eloquent testimony to the importance he places on the religious dimension of life. Jack evinces that peculiar bullishness, endemic to some pious people, that seeks to visit their individual personal truths on the rest of the human race. Jack is the recipient of a right-wing propagandist sheet, which escapes periodically from somewhere in Scotland, suggesting that the evils of the world, and especially those besetting the church, can invariably be traced to the radical propensities of either Darwin, Freud or Marx. Jack's agenda thereby receives fulsome confirmation and all kinds of imaginary windmills are tilted at: the advent of lay ministers of the Eucharist, the gimmickry of the modern liturgy, rampant sexual promiscuity, and so on. There is about Jack that dark Manichean inclination to postulate evil in whatever is not immediately reconcilable with his narrow, myopic view of life. The worries of the world are written all over his face, that constantly concerned look usually associated with grief or haemorrhoids.

'In the name of the Father and of the Son ...' Mickey Kearney has not arrived as yet. Even though the porch is crowded I miss the huge figure, arms carefully folded, a body language that displays a studied disregard for the proceedings. The whole point of his demeanour is to establish a certain agnostic distance from, if not rejection of, the ritual. Mickey would sympathise with Updike's view that churches bore the same relation to God as bill-boards did to Coca-Cola, promoting thirst without actually quenching it. The past, for him, is a foreign country and, even though he continues to defer to the social conventions of religious practice, it is an increasingly empty ritual. For him there is no detectable difference between believer and unbeliever. The rituals of Word and Sacrament are a kind of verbal music. Yet the presence of a priest is still confusingly reassuring – in Heaney's words:

Something in them would be ratified
when they saw you at the door in your black suit
arriving like some kind of holy mascot.

Leo Martin, on the other hand, has no such philosophical doubts. Not a man given to weighing the great metaphysical questions, he spends most mornings in bed, most afternoons watching television and most nights in a licensed establishment, playing darts and consuming vast quantities of alcoholic beverage. His income derives from the proceeds of an illicit distillery, unemployment assistance with a generous moiety in respect of the bevy of offspring he has, with his reluctant spouse, so assiduously propagated, and irregular excursions into what we call 'the black economy'. Leo could be described as one of the great supports of his local church or, more precisely, the back wall of his local church, with which he has over the years developed a special affinity. The extent of his religious commitment is that he confesses and receives once a year at the tail-end of the Easter season and, for the rest of the year, his is a vague presence in the vicinity of Sunday worship during which he is more liable to buy turf than to say prayers. Extraneous religious matters are the natural concern of his harassed spouse who, when not presiding with spectacular ineptitude over the tumult inflicted on the household by an indefinite number of offspring, is sampling the delights of bingo in the nearest market-town, or whatever alternative social occasion warrants an excuse for getting out of the house.

Pat Timlin needs to get out of the house too, but for very different reasons. A reluctant bachelor, he returned from England to care for ageing parents who disobliged his marriage prospects by surviving into their eighties. By then the girls he had, as he awkwardly put it, 'walked out with' were either married in Kent or waitressing in New York. Time or fate or God had predestined the unfortunate series of events that condemned him to looking into a lonely pint of Guinness every night of the week and finding his reluctant feet in the kind of bitter subculture Eugene McCabe captured so vividly in *King of the Castle*. Pat is a man without a past or a future. After several pints he can be coaxed into mulling over the experience of what Kavanagh

called 'the purgatory of middle-aged virginity' and the emotional
and sexual deprivation that attends it. Yet at Mass every Sunday,
Patrick is no reluctant observer, savouring as he does the richness of the ritual, understanding through it something of the
majesty and mystery of God and yet declining the invitation of
God's table, apart from the annual Easter duty on Trinity Sunday,
after a careful confession in Knock the day before.

George Crosby, on the other hand, attends and communicates
every Sunday. It would be unthinkable not to do so, a betrayal of
an ancestral loyalty. Sunday worship is an act of solidarity with
the community, a revered tradition validated by unbroken habit
and the blood of martyrs. George is of that strong Lisnagoola
tribe, the Cagaffs. Loyalty is their badge: to the GAA, where they
refuse to defer to the growing popularity of 'other codes'; to
Fianna Fail, to where an unbroken tradition is remorselessly defended in order to deflect any deviation from what de Valera
saw when he looked into his own heart; to the Roman Catholic
Church, where his conservative disposition and allegiance to
tradition find a comfortable home. George is of course also a
Pioneer, a Legionary of Mary, a caller of bingo numbers, a bearer
of clerical water and a hewer of clerical wood. It may be churlish
to say so, but George is also (let it be said) a veritable pain in the
neck, in that there is no crevice in his unimaginative mind
through which even the merest glimmer of compromise might
possibly filter. George's slit window is for him a boon, not a
limitation. His truth can be contained within rigid boundaries
and beyond that any unnecessary freedom to postulate alternatives simply confuses. For him – whatever about Newman's terse
injunction – to live well is not to change at all.

Patsy Cadden is not here. Retired and living alone, Patsy describes himself as an unbeliever, *rara avis ruri*, though there are
times on his long walks along the coastline when he admits to a
feeling of wonder and awe at the majesty and splendour of
creation. And I wonder sometimes is there any longer any detectable difference between him and, for example, Mickey
Kearney, he of the folded arms standing inside the back door in
a gesture, if not of defiance, at least of rejection. Has he 'the faith'
and Patsy not? Is it enough to parrot the words of the Creed once

a week as a verbal delineation of the boundaries of faith (as Mickey does), or is it ultimately a question of sensibility, a feel for the beyond in the bits and pieces of every day (as Patsy surely has)? Or is there a susceptible difference between a working faith and a true sense of God?

I wonder sometimes what brings Mickey to the church porch with such regularity and, at the same time, such ill-disguised disinterest in the proceedings. He is, after all, past the iconoclastic rumblings of youth that find expression in sharing with him for a while that draughty limbo at the end of St Brigid's. He is, too, as a self-possessed bachelor, unmoved by social pressure or the enforced religious conventions that family life demand. Is it no more than a vague deferral to an ancestral loyalty buried in a collective subconsciousness, the extended influence of a subversive Eucharist celebrated in some hidden glen? Or a studied reluctance to join the mass flight from reality into a temporary world of ritualised fantasy, *ignotum per ignotius*? Or a part payment to the ferryman, a mere sop to Cerberus? Or has it something to do with the great human hunger for hope, truth and goodness that impels his public, weekly narcosis? Could he say with Heaney,

> Give him his due, in the end
> he opened my path to a kingdom
> of such scope and neuter allegiance
> my emptiness reigns at its whim.

Or is that too much to hope for?

Occasionally on a dole-Tuesday, having taken St Paul's injunction *de vino* more seriously than the apostle surely intended, Mickey arrives, as local invective would have it, 'well cut'. Whereupon affairs of Church and State are aired for about an hour in something approaching an alcoholic haze. Advice is generously proffered on the content and length of my homilies, the state of the Church, universal and local, and the proclivities of human kind, general and particular.

Sins of calumny and detraction are committed all over the place with an abandon that in more innocent days we used to call 'gay'. And the resumé of every splintered reputation is concluded with the refrain 'the cute hoor', like a wayward chorus in some insignificant Greek drama. All the while his voice, guttural to an infuriating degree, waxes and wanes like a demented fund-amentalist preacher as he weaves the most ludicrous theories out of the most absurd premisses. I suffer on, in silence for the most part, and distract myself occasionally by imagining myself in a fit of rage throttling him and laying him out cold on the Axminster carpet. But that would be taking the business of creative counselling a bit far ...

Eventually Mickey will settle on his favourite theme which ex-plains (in so far as that's possible) his measured reluctance to go beyond the perimeter of the church. It has to do with his percep-tion of religion and religious as weak-willed, effeminate types who lack the vigour and passion of raw life, people whose spirit-uality emasculates them and who take refuge in longing for the fruits of another life, while the harvest of the present one is rot-ting all around them. I used to think that this antipathy to the feminine expressed a rural Irish version of the macho mentality, or an effort to seek personal affirmation of his bachelor ways, or even, God forgive me, something more sinister.

But when I watch him wobble his way home to Carrowhubbock on what used to be a bicycle, like an old cowboy riding precari-ously into the sunset, I sometimes think that he has something to say about the freedom of the children of God that is forgotten in the denial of life that sometimes disguises itself as a substitute for Christian living.

Ite, missa est.

IV Down all the days

After a few years in a parish, life acquires a certain rhythm. The idiosyncratic legacy of one's predecessor is gradually put in abeyance; the required expectations of parishioners are satisfactorily deprecated; and in the best parochial tradition, the pastor, having looked into his own heart, knows what is good for his people. The inevitable fact that it also coincides admirably with his own predilection is a not unexpected bonus. On the principle that 'I am an individual/ he is eccentric/ they are insane', giving the parish one's own stamp is an essential part of the settling-in process.

Weaning a full parish off the inherited wisdom of a past dispensation can be decidedly tricky, not to say wearying and time-consuming. Much of it depends on the energy and interests of one's predecessor. If through some unfortunate stroke of ill-luck he happened to be irredeemably smitten with the urge to leave some monument in cement to his memory, and succeeded in building a church or worse still a community centre, the task is well-nigh impossible. In this distressing situation, all one can hope for is a few controlled comments about the size of the debt (which implies a question-mark about the initial wisdom of the enterprise), some remarks about elephants (white) and herrings (red), and a prayer that the roof might consider springing an uncontrollable leak, preferably on the first anniversary of the never-to-be-forgotten opening ceremony.

If, as well as the aforementioned, he was an organisation freak, ineffably convinced that every committee in the parish, from the Dog-Show to the GAA, would instantly collapse without both his general enthusiasm and his particular charism as Chairman of this or Hon. Sec. of that, and if he had what is ambiguously called 'a way with the youth' and an appetite or aptitude for similarly exhausting enterprises, then the task is indeed impossible. And worst of all, if through neglect (understandable), or senility (incipient) or design (misguided), he allowed the parishioners some say in the running of the parish, then Aughrim is completely lost. Allowing the treasurer of the Board of Management of the national school to actually hold the cheque-book, or some rural feminist to insinuate herself into the Liturgy of the Word, or a choir to become so presumptuous as to suggest outrageously that the psalm might occasionally be sung, is a matter of slippery slopes, thin ends of wedges, not to speak of all manners of perfidious Albion or possibly Roma.

There are now, modern tradition has it, three kinds of parish. The first is where the writ of Vatican II runs, the second is where the writ of Vatican II will soon run, and the third is where those who do the running (or have the skids put under them) are those with the writ of Vatican II. And if perchance one inherited the latter from a judicious predecessor, the cup of parish life would surely run over. *O felix culpa.* Such an amenable circumstance might appear to demand nothing more exacting than benign dictatorship or palpable disinterest, but that is to underestimate the complicated procedures involved in inducing communal inactivity. What presents as thinly disguised idleness, or even lethargy on a grand scale, can be the result of complicated and demanding efforts to keep a situation in hand. The trick is to keep your distance without appearing aloof.

Reading the Word of God at Mass naturally presumes an adequate knowledge of the sociological and historical context, so the prerequisite of a primary degree in theology satisfactorily narrows the field in one fell swoop. (President of the Eucharistic Assembly – 1. People of God – nil.) The advent of lay ministers of the Eucharist would distress the faithful, and offertory processions are liturgically unacceptable in that they de-emphasise both Word and Eucharist. (P.E.A. – 3. P.O.G. – nil.) Access to the parish hall would necessitate an unwarranted insurance premium so, in the interests of both safety and economy, it may unfortunately be necessary to close it in the interim. Consequently the youth club, due to lack of suitable premises and a poor response for adult leaders, will not meet until further notice. (P.E.A. – 5. P.O.G. – nil.) And so on, hopefully *ad infinitum*. Nothing more ambitious than a necessary transmutation of an old concept, *l'etat c'est moi*, into a new context, *Ego sum parochia*.

This is what psychologists call the Education-Enlightenment hypothesis: the theory that convinces us that by telling people what makes good sense to us (or what we want) it will automatically make good sense to them. Supply the right information, give the right instructions and people become so enlightened that they will carry out your wishes to the letter. And despite the esoteric reservations of psychologists, the education-enlightenment theory works a treat, at least in a parish.

And so in time, parish life acquires a certain 'rhythm'. To such a degree that what the uninitiated might regard as 'unenlightened despotism' contrives to produce nothing that could possibly disturb the simplicity of faith or tranquillity of life that both defines a rural parish and contents its ageing pastor. But just as the most determined cultivation of chaos cannot prevent the occasional outbreak of order, so the most creative control cannot avoid the intermittent skirmish. Leaving aside the occasional anarchist who favours the purveying of confidential information – like what money is in the parish account – among the general populace, or the amateur theologian who believes mischieviously or impertinently that the phrase 'the Church is the people' could be held to justify some kind of mass involvement in parish affairs, the main areas of contention in rural parish life have to do with the Stations, announced Masses and baptisms.

'Stations' or neighbourhood Masses, as they are known to our revered city confères, who like a lot of other things mistakenly believe they invented them, have been part of rural parish life for centuries. Rather than manifesting any marked enthusiasm for the novel, they represent in effect something of a maintenance effort. For instance, there is no silence like the silence which descends on a Station house when the pastor enquires as to whose turn is next. And when, through a mixture of pressure or embarrassment – or ostentation if a new bungalow has just been built – someone is prevailed upon to host a Eucharist in six months' time, that decision, which to the initiated might seem curiously innocuous, contains within it the seeds of considerable annoyance. Invariably it will have to be postponed at least once due to some belated delinquency or other on the part of some local interior decorator, or the vague possibility that Aunt Katie might travel from Birmingham for the occasion. Then there is the great question as to whether morning or evening, Friday or Saturday, would be more suitable. Invariably, too, everyone wants a Saturday and in the distressingly casual, not to say in-disciplined, atmosphere of modern parish life there seems to be an increasing reluctance to accept in this matter, as in others, the accumulated clerical wisdom of the past. The laity in recent years, oblivious of the fact that the generic term which describes them is a synonym for non-professional, seem to be developing a distressing propensity for disbelieving that the clergy know better. Indeed in my own experience I have heard a religious, fresh from a course in that mythic notion called Collaborative Ministry, develop in this context a proposition that had echoes of the old principal of subsidiarity. In the event I had some diffi-culty convincing her that, though her theory had some merit in the area of theology, it was quite inappropriate in that it didn't apply to the Church.

Announced Masses constitute another minefield. It's one thing to pray for the dead; it's another to let the neighbours know you're doing it. An announced Mass on Sunday fulfils both a social and religious requirement. For that reason a premium is set on the main Sunday Mass, though unfortunately this is not always reflected in the stipend. Everyone wants it and if every-one doesn't get it a certain tetchiness has been known to creep into the discussion. Some arrive breathless on Saturday night convinced that they deserve special consideration in deference to the fact that it's their mother's anniversary and they hap-pened to forget all about it. Others suggest that their demands could be easily facilitated by shifting someone else's Mass, that was booked six months earlier, to 'some day during the week'. And most seem incapable of comprehending the huge responsi-bility of the *pro populo* obligation.

Indeed when I first came to Lisnagoola, I discovered to my horror that my predecessor actually encouraged the distraction of announced Masses on Sunday. To offset that wearying custom, I announced that heretofore the only intention on a Sunday would be the *pro populo* Mass. While I explained the canonical and other exigencies of this obligation at some length, I had the feeling that the wisdom I was so tortuously sharing was not being adequately grasped by the congregation. This fear was realised when, having turned down a request for an announced Sunday Mass, I was rather pointedly asked the identity of the Italian personage, *Pro Populo*, for whom I was saying Mass every Sunday! The same individual, I later learned, had for some unexplained reason an antipathy to Italians. Indeed, his espousal of a campaign to further the canonisation of Matt Talbot led him, on one memorable occasion, to confront some Padre Pio enthusiasts with the remark that 'if his protege was called Matteo Talbato and had several gloves, he's be canonised long ago.'

But where was I? Oh! yes. Even the official time of baptism can cause some disquiet. I sometimes envy our city confrères whose multiple baptisms not just earn them such 'merit' but more importantly necessitate an immutable schedule. It is difficult to be dogmatic when requests for the sacraments only occur every few months. Consequently baptisms are consistently requested at the most inconvenient times, like after dinner on a Sunday, when the prandial fruit of the vine is just about to induce a welcome siesta after the morning's exertions. This time is specially chosen to obviate the necessity for preparing a substantial meal for the guests, to facilitate such spurious and mysterious considerations as 'the time of the baby's feed', and to disrupt the quiet enjoyment of the *Beethoven Concert* from Vienna or *The Big Match*.

In my declining years, when the demise of concupiscence will have been celebrated and the ominously empty years of retirement will have me swaying perilously over the great chasm of boredom or senility, casting myself in the role of an Athanasius *contra mundum* I would hope to write a Pastoral Directory on avoiding the implementation of Vatican II. It would constitute a necessary balance for that deprived generation who had all this anarchy thrust on them from the breast, to help them remember what we went through to become what they are, what we once were until they knew better.

On current trends, it could be something of a best-seller, a *vademecum* for clerical rednecks. To offset the distressing popularity of recent publications that carry the torch for the vision of Vatican II, like *Alive, Alive O!*, I would call it *Dead as Doornails* with *une paroisse morte*, Bernanos' memorable phrase, as a subtitle. It would contain a long introduction explaining how the concept of *Pobal Dé* preceded the wisdom of the last Council and how the clergy in those unexciting years had little difficulty in disabusing that phrase of any substance. This telling thesis would be followed by reports from rural parishes which have retained the glorious inertia, the *festina lente* of the past, with illustrations featuring sanctuaries that still retain traditional altars, communion-rails and other Tridentine artefacts. Suggestions would be offered on ways of directing the energy of female iconoclasts into the altar society, and on the need for a genuine *laissez-faire* philosophy of parish, as distinct from such pastoral novelties as 'structured development based on analysis of the present situation'. And finally an appropriate Afterword could be supplied by some theologian-sociologist who could be given an acceptable conclusion and told to devise a survey to confirm it.

Part of the difficulty with enthusiasts of Vatican II is that they refuse to accept, even sometimes comprehend, one of the central truths of the pastoral scene, namely, that there is, in effect, nothing much to do. Most rural pastors are, thank God, wedged between two great chasms of what contrives to present itself as idleness, doing nothing and having nothing to do. Thus, enthusiasts of the latest Council discomfort us by striving to devise strategies to rescue us from this idyllic clime. It is not that the sheer and effortless banality of life deserves to be dignified by attributing to it an almost philosophical dimension, but that to function properly within the constraints of a quiet unique pastoral situation deserves a nod, if not a wink, in the direction of that central truth: most of us, most of the time, have little or nothing to do.

A colleague *sotto voce* confided to me recently that while hearing confessions during Holy Week in the Cathedral town, he was confronted by a quite insoluble problem. An elderly lady asked whether she might put him a question. Certainly, delighted and so on. 'Could you tell me, Father,' she meekly enquired 'something I've always wondered, how do ye spend the day?' Without putting too fine a point on it, my friend was flummouxed. Because, like the theology of the Trinity, the whole thing ultimately ends up in mystery. It is only in the secrecy of the confessional that such a question could be asked. More publicly we assent to the popular conspiracy among the devout and the sycophantic to convince us that we have a lot to do. 'You're very busy this last while, Father,' when a baptism and a funeral coincide in the same month. While our city colleagues, so busy that their black suits have faded into grey, try desperately to fit work to time, the rural brethren have the embarrassing luxury of fitting time to work.

So we devise strategies to fill the day. Some breed horses, or occasionally dogs, and deflect the ineffable tedium of their lives by going on irregular pilgrimages, horsebox and all, to insignificant gymkhanas. Others develop an emotional attachment to motor vehicles and spend most of their time visiting garages, the length and breadth of Ireland, where exotic models are continually priced and occasionally purchased. More become quiz freaks, spending most of their waking hours arranging obvious questions in order of triviality and acting as MCs at an embarrassingly endless series of question-times, table quizzes or, worse still, *Scór*.

Some become bingo enthusiasts, adept at organising that peculiarly obtuse pastime of chain-smoking buxom matrons, their nefarious offspring and depressed spouses, experts in the contorted minutiae of 'houses', 'lines' and 'jackpots' and oblivious to the progressive cerebral debilitation of listening to an endlessly unvarying repertoire of 'legs eleven' (11), 'top of the house' (90) and 'Downing Street' (10). Others again become honorary officers of the GAA, train the juveniles, organise the *Scór* competitions, assume the heavy mantle of Oifigeach na Gaeilge and whatever office would otherwise remain vacant, and become liable for the myriad other duties associated with that socio-religious-politico-athletic institution.

The golf course beckons others, and one of life's most debilitating illnesses quickly ensues – an obsession with detailing insignificant rounds of golf to the postman, milkperson or ESB
meter-reader, or whatever unfortunate has the patience to listen
or the misfortune to be caught. More become health-freaks,
berating their unfortunate parishioners with details of their personal menus, the benefit of an early-morning consumption of a
given combination of a dizzying variety of inedible cereals, the
deleterious effects of coffee and tea, and the merits of Tipperary
water.

Others jog, become addicted to the telephone, produce plays,
scour the death-notices to find a funeral to attend, do cross-
words, travel the world, watch television, become sleepolics and
other kinds of olics, attend every meeting, play the piano,
become cattlejobbers and sometimes tanglers, wait around for
others to make things happen so that they can go to them, or occasionally develop an interest in theology, say ecumenism or a
curiosity about the Arian controversy in the fourth century.

But what about parish work, *cura animarum* and all that? In truth,
for all intents and purposes it scarcely exists, except perhaps on
weekends. For the reason that there are few people. The young
are at school (and aren't the teachers wonderful?), the young
adults are in London and New York (and don't the emigrant
chaplains look after them?), the old are at their firesides (and
aren't they saying their prayers?). The middle-aged are mainly
settled couples and bachelors. Marriages run at two a year,
funerals at twenty, baptisms at six, confessions twice a year.
Then there's Christmas and Easter and First Holy Communion:
in all about a month's work. We are, whisper it so gently, (and
God bless James Larkin) the first generation of Irishmen to work
a two-day week.

Or has this always been the case? If it's possible to close down
the shop from Monday to Friday – a practice which is becoming
increasingly popular, especially for curates who have somewhere to go – if most of us find it difficult to find anything to do,
what of our predecessors? At least now there is the diversion of
organising readers, lay ministers, offertory procession, bidding

prayers and a sermon for the weekend Masses. In the Latin past, we turned our backs to the people, rarely preached or had to distribute Communion, and had everyone in and out before you could say Jack Robinson or Bob's your uncle. We were conscious, of course, at that idyllic time, of Fr Felix Zualdi's celebrated quote in that esteemed publication, *The Sacred Ceremonies of Low Mass*:

> 'The greater number of authors, incuding Benedict XIV, Clement IX, and other very learned pontiffs, declare that the celebration of the Sacrifice of the Mass should not occupy more than half an hour, nor less than the third part of an hour.'

As well as that, the *ex opere operato* maxim provided an amenable theology, the Roman vestments lasted for centuries, and there wasn't even heat in the church to turn on or off.

Now at least the Holy Week ceremonies, no matter how inadequately executed, demand at least minimal organisation; then, they hardly existed at all. Now presacramental preparation – Baptism, First Confession, First Communion, Confirmation and Marriage – necessitates the expenditure of some energy; then, it didn't exist at all. Now there is a Board of Management for the National School; then, none at all. Now continual visits to the young horrors; then, the teacher came to the presbytery, back door of course, to get the salary form signed. Now organisations and consequently meetings proliferate; then, just the Pioneers after last Mass on the First Sunday of the month. Before travel and television, how did they spend the day? *Quanta qualis errant illa sabbata.*

My point, which I grant has had an unusually tortuous gestation, is that little wonder I or my rural confrères should while away the days and months and years fantasising about – well, let's see – that red-buttoned soutane with the scarlet flaps, the definitive badge of our august Chapter, or whatever other fantasies are permitted within the narrow limits of the commandments and the even narrower confines of the statutes. *Vos valete et plaudite.*

V Doomed to do the decent thing

Winter is a depressing time. Furtive glimpses of spring breaking through the fog and frost of winter titillate the senses and then disappear, illusive shadows on the hoary wasteland. A good time for visiting, the penetrating cold restrains the seasonal temptation to linger along the hillsides tumbling with green growth in summer or retiring with russet stealth in autumn.

In winter, the trudge from home to home has its own rewards with the rich promise or threat of steaming tea and joyous turf-fires, anthems of a summer's labour, and above all, time, that declining commodity, an unexpected fruit of winter in rural Lisnagoola.

But perhaps, if the truth were told, it is a combination of guilt and the sight of a desk piled with the tumuli of ageing documents – mostly unopened circulars from the Department of Education – that drives me to irregular splurges of visitation. After the Eucharist, I believe it to be my most valuable work. Yet I often feel defeated by the ineffable tedium of the exercise, the long tortuous conversations about the weather or the virtues (mainly) of my predecessors, and the unrestrained chorus of cups of strong tea. Some prattle on about operations or medical histories, bad chests or wonky kidneys that disturb the even tenor of their lives. Others sit embarrassed by my presence, or the state of the house, in a silence like a deep well from which words can only be extracted with great effort. Time is the great gift to the lonely who spill out the pitiful discomforts that stalk their lives and imprison their minds; to women trapped in loveless marriages who lament the misery with which one irrational decision has visited their lives; to the widow who needs a listening ear as she recounts *ad nauseum* the circumstances of his death; to aged spinsters living on the memories of other days, faded photographs on a mantlepiece of a priest-uncle in America, dead for donkey's years; to settled bachelors lamenting a life which time and circumstances contrive to fashion into little more than thinly-disguised envy and incipient alcoholism; to those expecting me, in Heaney's phrase, 'to raise a siege the world had laid against their kitchen grottos'. All human life is there, the placid acquiescence of the contented, the corrosive cynicism of the disenchanted, the speculative questioning of the occasional agnostic, and, above all, the reverential awareness of God that somehow seems part of the landscape of life in Lisnagoola.

By including in the Sunday notices my intention to visit a particular townland, I both preclude alarm that a relative had died in England or America, once my Corolla is seen pulling into the haggard, and counteract my curious disinclination to move out of the house during the football season. Home visitation, unlike doing good or loving your neighbour, is distressingly quantifiable. 'Taking a run at it', in the conventional sense, is part of the secret. It's a dull grind at the best of times: saying the same things about the same subjects (weather, ill-health, teenagers, neighbours); offering reassurance about the state of the house or the future of the world; consuming vast quantities of strong tea and retreating home exhausted, like the proverbial nuns' confessor 'stoned to death with cornflakes'. Paul Durcan's *Tullynoe: Tête-a-Tête in the Parish Priest's Parlour* comes to mind, capturing as it does the empty echoes of an often surreal conversation:

> 'Ah, he was a grand man.'
> 'He was: he fell out of the train going to Sligo.'
> 'He did: he thought he was going to the lavatory.'
> 'He did: in fact he stepped out of the rear door of the train.'
> 'He did: he must have got an awful fright.'
> 'He did: he saw that it wasn't the lavatory at all.'
> 'He did: he saw that it was the railway tracks going away from him.'
> 'He did: I wonder if ... but he was a grand man.'
> 'He was: he had the most expensive Toyota you can buy.'

'He had well, it was only beautiful.'
'It was: he used to have an Audi.'
'He had: as a matter of fact he used to have two Audis.'
'He had: and then he had an Avenger.'
'He had: and then he had a Volvo.'
'He had: in the beginning he had a lot of Volkses.'
'He had: he was a great man for the Volkses.'
'He was: did he once have an Escort?'
'He had not: he had a son a doctor.'
'He had: and he had a Morris Minor too.'
'He had: he had a sister a hairdresser in Kilmallock.'
'He had: he had another sister a hairdresser in Ballybunion.'
'He had: he was put in a coffin which was put into his father's cart.'
'He was: his lady wife sat on top of the coffin driving the donkey.'
'She did: Ah, he was a grand man.'
'He was: he was a grand man ...'
'Goodnight, Father.'
'Goodnight, Mary.'

Being there is what matters. Visitation indicates an acceptance of, availability to and concern for people in a way that all the verbalising in the world cannot do. It's priesting, shepherding at its most basic, and all it demands is patience, a thick skin and a good constitution. Talent of any description is unnecessary for this priestly test and those who persevere get full marks from their people.

Fortunately, there are occasional lapses from the definitive tedium of the experience. Jack Killeen, living on his wits and yet another illicit distillery, is a case in point. A bachelor cum rural entrepreneur, he has wedded an ancient custom (poteen-making) and the new technology (cylinder gas) with such success that he has become his own greatest customer. A natural raconteur, his thatched cottage has become a kind of miniature community centre, even though the atmosphere seems always to be compounded of equal proportions of alcohol and smoke. On my first visit, in an effort to be agreeable at all costs I sampled a modicum of his product, throwing it back as he did in time-honoured fashion, like a cowboy in a saloon. It had the same effect as putting my head in a press and asking Mike Tyson to slam the door.

In Mary Conlon's, the atmosphere is, in many ways, less liberal. Mary is of the old school, lamenting the demise of Benediction and the Latin Mass, decrying 'this modern fad' of lay readers and the outrage of lay ministers. Once an Amazonian worthy of legendary proportions, she now cuts a sad figure as arthritis takes its toll. What energy she has is now devoted to corresponding with various friars who, to my practised eye, are regularly relieving her of large portions of her considerable fortune. She seems to be blithely unaware that the parish of Lisnagoola or its hard-pressed pastor could well do with some of her largesse. Various hints to this effect have been singularly ineffective. Indeed, I have often felt – particularly when she holds forth about poor Fr Athanasius taking a welcome break in one of the Order's continental watering-places – that a more frontal approach may be appropriate. Every month Mary presents me with the latest edition of the Order's publication, a poor production that seems to be based on the principle that if you repeat clichés with sufficient passion you can end up sounding profound. Mary is peculiarly worried about the promiscuity of the modern generation, a passion which she apparently shares with Fr Athanasius. Large stipends are apparently forced upon him for Masses to make reparation for 'those terrible sins'.

After Mary Conlon, Brogans is a welcome relief from the weariness of worrying about the state of the world. At the last count, there were eleven young Brogans and they scurry in different directions as I enter. A lighthearted remark at a recent baptism about 'making it the round dozen' didn't go down very well. Being the kind of person who wouldn't see the cracks on the ceiling until the house fell in, Winnie Brogan has recently been converted to the unreliability of Natural Family Planning. After her fifth child, my predecessor – who knew about all this and often expatiated in dizzying detail about it as if it were some kind of biological traffic-lights with red signals and green signals – had apparently encouraged her in that orthodox direction and now, six children later, she attributes its failure and her predicament to the Church, or, rather unfairly I thought, to me as its more obvious representative. Her life seems to be one long battleground of sleepless nights, dirty nappies and regurgitated cornflakes.

Her husband, Jacko, sits smoking the pipe, ensconced in an armchair whose seat seems to have collapsed under his oppressive weight. This gives him an eerie appearance as his head is roughly level with his knees, and his occasional monosyllabic contributions to the conversation, which Winnie invariably seems to interpret as approval, seem to come from the bowels of the earth. He sits impassively between two bags of turf which remind me vaguely of votive offerings at the feet of a pagan god, and he just pulls away on the pipe and looks into the fire as Winnie holds forth on the limitations of what she called NFP. On one visit, to deflect the conversation somewhat, I motioned to a huge gaudy trophy that dominated the mantelpiece. In the event this was a masterpiece of distraction, as Winnie suddenly lost interest in NFP and began to hold forth on Jacko's prowess at darts. Whereupon Jacko, looking for all the world like an icon, hauled himself to his feet, a process that consumed most of the afternoon, and took down the trophy, holding it carefully in his hands as if it were a Fukien figurine from the early Ming dynasty. The children, who were swarming over me like American GI's trying to retake Pork Chop Hill, suddenly descended on Jacko and his trophy, and he beat them off with a mixture of threat and promise. *Exegi momumentum aere perennius.* Obviously poor Horace never got as far as Brogans. Eventually I escaped, relieved that Winnie hadn't insisted I stay for supper, and promising myself that in the future I would resist my uneasy urge to pontificate on the joys of family life.

Next door, Chuck, a recent immigrant from America, welcomes me profusely. He has, he tells me, some difficulty understanding the peculiar customs of the Irish. These seem to centre mainly on when we get up, when we go to bed and when we get around to doing what we said we would do yesterday. The culture shock has to do with Church too. The November offerings for the dead, Mass-cards, station dues, stole fees, plate and harvest collections, form an idiosyncratic maze that does not easily admit of

clear explication. Despite my best efforts and Chuck's disturbing penchant for interspersing the conversation with remarks
like 'Wow, you gotta be kidding' and 'Gee, Father, that's for the
birds', the subject became, if anything, less clear. Amazingly,
Chuck found it difficult to understand that if he gave me a fiver
I'd say Mass for his dead but if he puts a fiver into the November
envelope I put it with someone else's fiver before a Mass is said.
A short sermonette on the indivisibility of the Mass, and a few
well-chosen words on the disturbing trend towards a mentality
of ownership over the Mass, were singularly ineffective. He also
found it difficult to understand how priests could live on their
meagre income.

I toyed momentarily with the possibility of suggesting to Chuck
that he develop his ideas further and visit the local ordinary, but
this former car salesman from the Bronx, with his unhappy combination of wordiness and theatricality, might not so much
break the mould of rural Church life as catapult his Lordship
into premature retirement. Besides, there was the distinct possibility that he might be asked what David prevailed on him to act
the part of Uriah the Hittite.

Chuck has also developed some novel ideas about improving
the quality of my sermons. They mainly involve what he calls
'the dialogue approach'. He would interrupt me from the body
of the congregation and I would reply. In this way, he says, we
'could get something going' and inject 'a bit of pizzazz' into the
proceedings. I find it difficult to convince him that Lisnagoola
might not be quite ready for such studied confrontation.

In much the same way, Lisnagoola hasn't taken to another of
Chuck's enthusiasms, what he calls 'jogging'. It's a kind of shuffle which, despite giving a great impression of movement, is in
fact much slower than walking. The secret is apparently to keep
at it until you collapse from sheer exhaustion, a form of
masochism something akin to the flagellantes in the Middle
Ages. Chuck's early morning jogs around the winding roads of
the parish, all sweat and heavy breathing, have done little to
convince locals either of its appeal or of his sanity. In an effort to
add a note of levity to the discussion, I suggested that it seemed

more a psychological illness than a form of exercise but my opinion was instantly disallowed on the irrefutable ground that some priest in New York regarded it as a religious, possibly mystical experience.

My visits to Chuck induce a medley of conflicting emotions: depression, in that his sheer exuberance and openness evinces, on my part, not support or encouragement but a devastating caution; exhilaration in that this foreign iconoclast, totally oblivious of rural religious formalities, would do such outrageous things as answer the response at Mass and actually sing in the choir. Above all, calling on him is a welcome change from the attitude of mystified reverence or the traditional sycophancy that home visitation normally elicits. Exceptional occasions in the dull grind of home visitation are to be treasured.

Home visitation is probably the most valuable work a pastoral priest will do. It may not rank with the theological significance for priesthood of preaching God's word or administering the sacraments, and its import may be circumvented by the *ex opere operato* enthusiasts of the older school, but it remains, in an age excessively conscious of specialised expertise, a *sine qua non* for even minimal pastoral care. The value of tilling the field closest to home in the most traditional way is not a truth that excites anymore. It has not the *frisson* of ploughing new furrows every other week. My own conviction in the matter is reinforced by an episcopal injunction (whose every word and so forth) and the stipulations of the Maynooth Statutes, now regularly reviled but not, to my knowledge, abrogated. And there is, too, the not inconsiderable matter that, from time immemorial, it has been established as an effective pastoral practice. Indeed while Mahoney is 'loth to multiply grave obligations for the clergy, it is certain that episcopal laws may bind *sub gravi*' and O'Donnell recommends it highly:

> A priest must go down amongst his people, study their needs, their interests, their tendencies, their *differentia maxime propria*, observe their lives, their thoughts, their language, sympathise with their toils and temptations, and realise their joys and sorrows. It is friendly intercourse that breaks down

reserve and reticence and dissipates narrowness and angularity of view. When paying a visit, umbrella, goloshes and overcoat are left in the hall; but it is usual to retain one's hat, as a gentle reminder that a morning call is of brief duration.

Despite the obvious welcome of my flock and the pleasant chat about the weather and so forth, I remain very much a strange visitor from a foreign land. We sometimes delude ourselves into believing that as individuals we have become almost indispensable to parish or people. The longer the appointment, the more likely the delusion. Invariably when we move, we realise it was the office and not the man that mattered. There is, almost by definition, a perceptible distance between sheep and shepherd. Possibly it has to do with the cultic version of priesthood on which most are weaned. Or with its curious satellite, celibacy, or maybe our unrelievedly middle-class grooming. What is it about the effete idiosyncratic world we inhabit that prohibits us from tuning into the rhythms of our people? Bingo or bridge, turnips or ratatouille, *Newsnight* or *Glenroe*, *The Irish Times* or *Ireland's Own*? It is a matter of language, accent, taste, even aesthetics. And how to bridge that gap? How to tune into the insoluble complexities of ordinary life without patronising those to whom we minister? The gospel according to Jacko.

VI Musings on clerical life

Autumn is a season not just of mists and mellow fruitfulnesss but of dying days and drooping spirits as summer packs a last bag. The mood is sombre, melancholic, apposite to the approach of winter. Crops, wearily harvested in the dankness of a summer's labour, are secured in tidy haggards, fishing-nets ravaged by a season's work hang dejectedly in outhouses. The village's only Carpigiani, a great benign beast dutifully disgorging Italian-style ice-cream on summer Sundays, is in enforced hibernation at the rear of Devaney's shop. Even the children seem to droop in desolation under the weight of their school bags. And the rural pastor, like Ixion on his wheel revolving endlessly through the heavens, frets at the dulling prospect of the hard grind of another desolate winter. 'You won't find until the Stations', a parishioner remarks. Depression rules, okay.

How to ease the burden of nature's gloom? The Reverend Sydney Smith's antidote was a good, blazing fire. A more modern cleric might embellish that warming prospect with generous portions of *aqua vitae*. A genteel confrère, elegant to the point of foppishness, suggests his own idiosyncratic passion, rugmaking, which diversion is summarily dismissed by his macho colleagues as a glorified form of knitting. Others mend clocks, mount their exercise bicycles, trade antiques, fall in love with their computer, or jog. A better prospect might be an occasional walk by the sea, savouring the varied moods of Neptune, drawing solace from the perennial movements of land and seascape and communing with the irreducible forces of time and tide that, even in Lisnagoola, wait for no one.

Maybe it is the advent of late middle age rather than the coming

46

of winter that induces such melancholy. Or the feeling that the cup of life no longer runneth over, but that the sands of time are inexorably running out. We begin to fantasise about entering an enclosed order, or opting dramatically for the missions, somewhere demanding like Peru or more congenial like California. We experience an almost despairing need to drop some pebble into the tranquil pool of life. Perhaps we just reach that moment in life when apparently well-settled people are tempted to set out for a second visit to their youth. Gaugin gave up his comfortable life and set sail for Tahiti to paint his pictures. And most of us long to attempt a similar anabesis, however much we know we might regret arriving at our destination. Youth, indeed life itself, has been burgled by an unmemorable catalogue of activities that pass for treading the Way, but one longs occasionally for a gentler gradient.

With the oil of ordination scarcely dry on our hands, we embrace with enthusiasm, if not conviction, the minutiae of clerical life. We actually enjoy the weekly bingo session, acquire a facility for selling poolsheets or training the juveniles, and get a kick out of counting the collection. There follows a period of retrenchment, when we assess the fruits of all that energy, the burden of unfulfilled expectations and the quiet loneliness that is the birthright of the celibate. We recognise in retrospect the three definitive stages of settling into the priesthood. The first, polishing the chalice and the car; the second, polishing the car; and the third, polishing neither. And above all, we come to realise the folly of believing that we are valued for what we are rather than for what we do. Priesthood can take on the semblance of a life-sentence, and we are tempted to succumb to a state of lucid indifference. Some develop an emotional attachment to the telephone, others a terminal passion for golf, still others sink without trace before their televisions and become world authorities at tracing the narrative intricacies of *Neighbours* or *Coronation Street*, and all, of course, are converted to the convenient eighteenth century belief that a man of God can live both in comfort and good conscience.

Perhaps it is some kind of clerical midlife crisis. After all, some form of Promethean discontent inevitably characterises the human condition. And the Americans have found the word for it, *Burnout*. And just as they tend to turn every event into an occasion, it goes without saying that they turn every idea into a book or series of books. Burnout, if these transatlantic tracts are to be believed, is a form of exhaustion, a diminution of libido.

Behavioural scientists identify six typical symptoms of the burnout condition: difficulty in sleeping, lack of interest in food, gastro-intestinal disturbances, low-grade persistent depression, a nagging boredom, and a chronic tiredness. My own experience of clerical life would indicate that the condition is not thankfully widespread in Ireland. For a group who go to bed just to sleep, as a bishop said one time, we spend if anything an inordinate amount of time 'resting'. 'Lack of interest' would be a poor description of our attitude to food, and offhand I can think of several lethargic types who, in this regard, are notably not suffering from burnout. There are, to my knowledge, no statistics indicating the incidence of gastro-intestinal disturbances among the brethren, and apart from the occasional rumble *in extremis* there is no evidence that it has reached epidemic proportions. And of course, depression, boredom and tiredness are no more than inevitable consequences of the pastoral life, indeed in a sense basic requirements for priesthood.

The fact that it all sounds slightly daft is, however, no indication that burnout is not an accepted psycho-medical condition. And apparently priests, because of the nature of our work, are particularly prone to it. Our work is repetitive, never-ending, tedious and unquantifiable. Sisyphus is our reluctant model. People are demanding, inconsiderate, and some of them all of the time, and all of them some of the time, a veritable pain in the neck. A priest's life can so easily become a vast dumping ground for the pains, worries, frustrations of an entire parish. We can, as a result, spend much of our lives in a sea of guilt or doubt, occasionally coming up for air only to be carried under again by a new wave of depression and despair. Seminary training that stressed the 'Be ye perfect' model left little scope for those less than heavenly. The truth is that we all need a healthy regard for our own failure. It is so easy to develop a Curé d'Ars complex, or get carried away through an admirable though unreflective idealism and end up depressed and exhausted, desperately clinging to the remnants of our fading delusions about our capacity to change, if not the world, at least our own parish. Those who try to be all things to all men usually end up being very little to very few. And those who try to be all things to all women usually end up being everything to one or two.

The antidote to the burnout condition can take different forms. Of the three things every man wants to do in life, plant a tree, write a book and have a child, only the first is generally realisable by the brethren, though in exceptional circumstances ... Better, perhaps, to leave it at that. Creative activity, like gardening, carpentry or painting, feed what one book calls 'the exhausted ego'. Physical activity can also be helpful, the *mens sana in corpo sano* sort of thing, and should be engaged in as an enjoyable exercise rather than in the belief that, like celibacy, if something makes you feel terrible it must be doing you some good. Jogging can fit the bill, provided it is engaged in to such an extent that it produces, at the very least, bouts of heavy breathing. For obvious reasons and so as not to give scandal, it is perhaps better that this be a solitary activity and, if possible, it should be engaged in outside the parish. A neighbouring parish enjoys (if that's the right word) the daily sight of an extremely obese curate wobbling through the village like a blancmange in a panic, by common consent not a very pretty sight and, for some, even grossly disedifying. Days off should be absolutely sacrosanct on the grounds that work that is unduly repetitive needs to be systematically interrupted. Otherwise the feminine side of our nature, for those who have one, is perversely affected. We should refuse to allow others unload their guilt on us. We should refuse to allow our people to insinuate their expectations into our lives. And above all we should stop using the word *should*!

And finally, what are delightfully called 'creative relationships'. Human relationships, we're told, 'coagulate the personality', are 'creative sources of energy' and provide 'a vital outlet for our Eros'. I wouldn't doubt it for a second, but what this is Americanese for is not exactly clear. Possibly it refers to a colleague who, placid in personality and depressed by nature, after more than three decades of stodgy service in the priesthood, has recently swapped his soutane for a wardrobe of definitively florid proportions. He now disports himself in red tie and garish shirt in the local disco and is something of a kareoke favourite at the local watering-hole. In America they call it 'coagulating the personality' or 'rediscovering creative sources of energy'; in Ireland it's called 'losing the run of yourself'.

There is much discussion too about something called 'intimacy', 'repression impeding maturity', 'developmental celibacy', and what is mysteriously referred to as 'the third way'. God be with the days when particular friendships were frowned upon, *custos occulorum* was regarded as a vital cog in the spiritual machine, bad thoughts were more serious than sexual fantasies and persons of the opposite sex were canonically required to keep their distance, *solus cum sola*. Remember the Maynooth Statutes? Number Fourteen, Sub-section One to be precise :

> A priest shall altogether avoid familiar acquaintance, not to say intimacy with women, even devout women, especially *solus cum sola*.

I hesitate to mention number Sixteen, that under pain of suspension:

> A priest shall not retain any woman as a comrade in his own house … except for those connected to a priest by a rather close degree of consanguinity.

O tempora, o mores! How times have changed! Now, Maynooth Statutes notwithstanding (and I choose the word carefully), we are expected to give expression to the great human capacity for intimacy, encouraged to accept our physicality, respond to our fantasies, and generally behave as normal people. Celibacy, I somethimes think, is no problem once you accept the fact that it has less going for it than marriage.

Part of the problem may be the peculiar self-obsession that often attends clerical life. There is the perception, for instance, that every incident in clerical life is, by definition, of great consequence for most of Christendom. Coming up for air, as we only occasionally do out of a world equivalent to that of Barbara

Pym's *Fine Women*, it is unsurprising that we sometimes wonder whether any other world actually exists.

We are, at least in rural parts, surrounded by people who invariably, and often disingenuously, assure us about our relentless virtues. Consequently the temptation to confer significance on every word we say, every action we perform, every idea we birth, is not always successfully resisted. We ingest with the undiscerning milk of human kindness a resistance to perceiving reality as in the main insipid, bland, uninteresting and above all, 'ordinary', with, of course, a small 'o'. It may have something to do with an over-pious theology of priesthood, or overly-indulgent spiritual directors, or both. Every thought becomes a temptation, every appetite an occasion of sin, every meeting a Bergman-like game of chess for an immortal soul, and every conversation a homily. It presents as an inability to accept that life in the main is dull, repetitive, uninteresting, sad and essentially comic. Clerical life, like Irish sport, has its moments, and they have to be unambiguously cherished, but they are moments nonetheless. The clerical agenda is devastating in its ordinariness. The tide ebbs and flows on Lisnagoola Strand as it has done for centuries, and the incidents we imagine to be dramas interest no one but ourselves.

But we can take all of this too far. The freedom of God's children, which is our natural birthright, can be sacrificed on the absurd altar of minimalism. There is in clerical life a kind of cerebral wastage, a progressive diminishment of the mental faculties that debilitates even the most talented of men. There is a fossilisation that seems almost endemic to the clerical state, that can convert lively, enthusiastic and brilliant men into shufflers and fumblers and plodders.

In another existence, they would have written poetry, administered corporations, built skyscrapers and cheered anyone lucky enough to be in their company with a style and breadth of vision that owed less to education or formation than to the God who endowed them so profusely. In secondary school they were the cream of the class. In university they casually romped home with Firsts, or as near to Firsts as made no difference. And in theology they mesmerised the rest of us with a precise control of the minutiae of Canon Law.

But somewhere along the line, in parishes, after a lifetime of eating Station breakfasts, reading the *Irish Independent*, watching *Coronation Street* on television, and hauling bags of turf to the hob, something went awry. Lights went out somewhere. Bells stopped ringing. Some kind of deterioration took place. Men who went on annual pilgrimages to London to savour the delights of Covent Garden cannot now summon the interest to buy a new gramaphone and wouldn't recognise a C.D. if it attacked them in the street. Theatregoers, who on dangerous wintry nights regularly drove the length of Ireland and back to the Abbey to relish the presence of an F. J. McCormack or the studied wistfulness of a Siobhan McKenna, couldn't make it to the local hall if Our Lord himself was playing the main part in a Passion Play. Inveterate globetrotters, who so mastered the intricacies of foreign travel that they circled the globe on inadequate incomes, now have healthy bank balances but couldn't be prevailed upon to cross the road. Intellectuals, who delighted in the challenges to traditional wisdom presented by Bertrand Russell and Karl Rahner and the stimulus such conflict generated, have long ago stopped reading *The Furrow* and now make do with *The Irish Catholic*. Literati, who devoured the classics and were devoted to good books, flick absentmindedly through the only publication they now order, the bland fare of *The Reader's Digest*. And former avid students of pedagogy are gradually disappearing under a mountain of unopened brown envelopes bearing the legend *An Roinn Oideachais*.

What is happening to us? Is it old-age or burnout? Or the endlessly dreary weather, the mists wafting around us invading our souls and corroding our spirits? Or maybe it has to do with more than a modicum of self-pity when the seasonal warmth of family life seems curiously to exacerbate the emotional austerity of our celibate stables. If winter comes? We can at least look forward to the coming of another spring.

VII Curates and their curiosities

In the few months since Fr Derek's arrival, *per Deum et episcopum*, to these shallow pastoral waters, we have built something of a relationship out of a series of precursory skirmishes which served to define certain pastoral, liturgical, even physical boundaries, a ritual (now that I think about it) not unlike the mating pattern of the African mongoose. A discussion, say, of the Holy Week ceremonies will have Derek sounding off about some esoteric liturgy during which, in his previous incarceration, he washed the feet of several nuns. I relate a story about a priest somewhere in the Midlands who was reputed, on a similar occasion, to have washed the feet of six men and the hands of six women, and go on to reminisce at some necessary length on the solemnity and reverence of the erstwhile Cathedral *Tenebrae*. No buckets or saucepans liturgy there, mind you. Indeed it was possible to nod off for considerable periods and not really miss anything.

I detect a certain impatience with, if not rejection of, my operational thesis that the less people know the more they appreciate. This principle, which over the years has served me admirably, not least in the delicate matter of parish finances, Derek apparently finds distinctly unconvincing. To illustrate his point, he meanders through several documents of the most recent Council alluding to 'the mind of the Fathers', 'the working of the Holy Spirit' and his own particular expertise in a dizzying variety of associated areas. Shades of Goldsmith's teacher:

> And still they gazed and still their wonder grew
> That one small head could carry all he knew.

I counter with a few well-chosen words on the value of tradition, the danger of excessive enthusiasm and some solid 'stuff' from

Noldin and Van Noort. He affects a belief that the latter gentlemen were really Dutch footballers in heavy disguise and laughs
uproariously at his own joke. I respond by accepting that while
this is, as Pius X put it, 'the age of the lay apostolate', and while I
accept Archbishop Ireland's remark that 'Active laymen are particularly needed in the Church today', it is the constant 'praxis'
(that impressed him) of the Church to move slowly, deliberately
and prudently. Whereupon he looks into the distance and mut-
ters something about something called 'inclusive language'. It's
that kind of dance, two steps out and one step in again.

In our varied skirmishes no blood, so to speak, has as yet been
drawn. We have both mastered the technique of indirectly stalk-
ing the prey, defining the boundaries of what is mutually acceptable, avoiding contentious areas where elements of preju-
dice, self-esteem and interest can ferment into lethal potions,
and drawing thin lines between the possible and the probable,
the idealistic and the achievable.

Curates, it is clear, are no longer a predictable species. *Tempora
mutantur nos et mutamur in illis*. In the tranquil past they arrived
from the seminary black-suited, starchly Roman-collared, cleric-
ally stocked, white cuffed, shoes shining and the inevitable
Pioneer pin: all swathed in a black gaberdine overcoat that came
below the knees, like the famous advertisement for McCaul's
Clerical Outfitters on the back of *Christus Rex*.

In the good old days curates looked decent, scrubbed, exquisitely
carbolic. The sort of priest you could confidently introduce to a
reverend mother, or safely to your housekeeper. They drove
black Volkswagens, owned black leatherbound breviaries with
zips around the edges, and wore brown scapulars around their
necks. Their great ambition in life was to become a parish priest
and their greatest asset was that they knew no theology. For example, they didn't know the difference between canon law and
moral theology, rubrics and liturgy, Marbella and the Costa del
Sol, and their ignorance stood them in good stead. For them the
bishop was the only official visionary in the diocese and the PP
the only person who really mattered. You kept clear of the former and you sought, with varying degrees of success, some

modus vivendi with the latter. God was in his heaven, the bishop was in his palace and the PP was in charge.

'Carbolic' is not the first word that comes to mind with Fr Derek. He is of a different vintage, literally and metaphorically. On his first visit, he was dressed in what looked like badly shaped pyjamas, but which I have since discovered is his Sunday suit, designed at apparently colossal expense by a Mr Louis Copeland from Dublin. He was afraid, he confided to me later, after consuming an inordinate quantity of my Remy Martin, that he was on that occasion overdressed. *Fieri non potest ud idem sentiant qui aquam et qui vinum bibant.* Underdressed stretched to a tracksuit and sneakers in outrageous colours which made him look like one of those revoltingly healthy participants in a TV ad for a new margarine.

At the time and while the subject was raised, I felt it encumbent on me as his canonical superior to acquaint him with a past issue of the now unhappily defunct *Irish Ecclesiastical Record*. Some canonical luminary responded to the question as to whether there was any obligation in conscience always to wear clerical dress, and whether there were any sanctions attached to the law. The question was, apparently, inspired by a rumour, and it was no more than that, that in the 1930s some priests on holidays were discarding clerical attire. The gist of the reply was that, in conscience, the obligation of wearing clerical dress is a grave one, that is to say 'its non-observance is a mortal sin'. Canon E. J. Mahoney in his inestimable work, *Priests' Problems*, confirms this prognosis and, while he goes on to say that the law, while grave in itself, does admit smallness of matter in respect to the period during which it is not observed, St Alphonsus is credited with permitting in certain circumstances a continuous period of no more than six days. Also, certain kinds of illness, presumably those involving hospitalisation, may demand a form of relaxation unattainable while dressed as a cleric. Thomas O'Donnell too, in his *The Priest of Today: His Ideals and His Duties*, has some salutary comments to make:

> The dress and outward bearing of a priest should correspond
> with his serious and sacred character. The newest fashions in

dress, showy ornaments, hair cultivated with feminine solicitude, such things are … out of harmony with the simple propriety of the priest. If a priest is foppish people regard him as vain.

Simplex cultus capillorum, as Canon 1436 has it. Indeed, a decree of the Third Council of Baltimore runs as follows:

> We order clerics when at home or in the church to wear a soutane and when in public intercourse with the world to wear such a dress as will by its length and dark colour distinguish them from the laity.

'That's my tartan kilt out the window so', was Fr Derek's giddy response, though he did show a particular interest in borrowing the books I mentioned so that he could discuss them with his class-mates.

'Car-wise', to use his own phrase, Fr Derek drives a turbo-diesel Peugeot 405, often at wanton speed through my front gates, with little apparent sense of the havoc he might one day wreak on PP, housekeeper or garden gnome. He talks about it endlessly, explaining that even though it cost the earth, a whole series of variables meant that he got it for half nothing, the endemic self-deception of the motoring enthusiast.

There were other enthusiasms too. In an effort to help me appreciate how inadequate it was to his needs, he gave me a guided tour of his four-bedroomed house. He called it 'an exercise in practical conscientisation'. I would call it an education. Placed randomly around one room were a personal computer (his PC) cum word processor with a CD-ROM and multi-media facility, a high resolution graphics monitor, a daisy-wheel printer, screen filter, copystand, an acoustic hood sound control unit, diskette holders, printout binders, a scanner and several operating manuals. It was, he told me, all IBM compatible (at which I nodded uncomprehendingly) and its main function was in data-processing. It would all, he assured me, save enormous amounts of time.

How he would spend the time saved was obvious in the next room. Here there was a television, a video, a stereo music centre with compact disc facility, a tape-deck and four-band radio. There were library units for his collection of video tapes, audio tapes and records, though with the advent of the compact disc (his CD), the latter were now (he said) 'technologically obsolete qualitywise'. I wasn't quite sure what that meant but it seemed to be something he regretted. All of this equipment seemed to be intricately interconnected, could be activated by a sophisticated remote-control gadget and, with speakers placed strategically around the house, reproduced an even distribution of sound in every room including the toilet (his WC, I presume). To experience the overall effect, he played a song entitled *The Oldest Swinger in Town* and I had to traipse around the whole house. His bedroom was a sight to behold. A large teddy-bear was placed in the centre of the bed and several other furry siblings were placed randomly around the room. Along each wall was a chorus of shoes in all shapes, styles and sizes, a selection that might even take Imelda Marcos's breath away. Clearly, I thought to myself, the centipede had insinuated himself into his genetic avenue, somewhere along the ancestral line. His bathroom contained enough towels to dry half the parish and contained such an array of toiletries,

> And now unveiled the toilet stands displayed
> Each silver vase in mystic order laid

that I began to wonder whether there was some anatomical equivalent of the Amazon basin which pre-Vatican II clergy had not as yet discovered.

I suggested, obliquely I hope, that a priest's house should be, as O'Donnell puts it, 'an example to others of Christian becomingness and decorum'. While a priest was clearly entitled to a reasonable level of comfort, including reasonable attention to all the canons of sanitary science, at the same time modesty, moderation and prudence should prevail. I reminded him that a previous Ordinary in the diocese had rejected the proposal to erect a lavatorial convenience in a parish house on the anatomically curious, but canonically defensible, grounds that the encumbent was merely a curate. It was too, I pointed out, in a climate particularly unsuitable to early morning visits to the end of the gar-

den. Fr Derek, as was his wont, missed the point completely and
insisted on topping my little interlude with his own story of an
Irish father whose son wrote to him from Wisconsin with the
confusing news that in America they eat in the garden and
defecate in the house, while the Irish pattern was quite the opposite. Yet O'Donnell's counsel deserves attention:

> Apart from the ordinary principles of sanitation, the general
> character of a priest's home should be marked by simplicity
> and a certain amount of religious feeling. Hence, in size and
> style, it should be unpretentious, not provoking unfriendly
> comment nor exceeding the moderate requirements of one
> who has left all things to follow Christ. Ornaments should be
> plain and solid, furniture not extravagant, and pictures and
> prints not of a kind to offend the eyes of modesty.

Theologically, my altercation with Fr Derek was an uneven contest. Derek is an intelligent man, has an obsession with the most
recent Council, and has an irredeemably serious side to his nature, an ominous cocktail. It is probably my own creaky theological credentials that account for my failure to swim across the
intellectual moat with which he manages to surround every
theological topic. He has, too, a distressing habit of giving sermonettes to update me in this or that area, peppering his remarks
with obscure jawbreakers, which if I knew enough, I could dismiss as jargon. He mentions a journal called *Concilium* quite
often, a set of volumes called *Theological Investigations*, and a
deceased German Jesuit called Karl Rahner.

I enjoy reminding him that, to my knowledge, Karl Rahner was
never in Lisnagoola and he responds by once again looking
vaguely into the distance, indicating at least mild exasperation
or, at most, controlled condescension. It would be unfair to ac-
cuse him of anything as outrageous as intellectual arrogance,
though in all honesty he evinces occasionally the kind of hubris
that PPs take a lifetime to cultivate, but that theology professors
seem to manage in three weeks. He is of course a 'conservative
liberal' as distinct from a 'liberal conservative', in that tradition
is more a taste than a conviction, a subtle garnish rather than the
main course.

What's particularly disconcerting – theology being not that relevant to life here – is that this attitude spills over into pastoral affairs. Tried and tested conventions are perceived as no more than a challenge to his reforming spirit. Upsetting the settled etiquette of clerical life induces a certain anarchic delight. Derek has for instance, a certain difficulty with the parish hall, an unease with a seeming conflict between him running it, and me telling him what to do. He evinces a certain distaste for clerical titles and seems to hold the Diocesan Chapter – which I personally hope one day to join – in particularly low esteem. He lacks the ambition to serve a long apprenticeship for the high office of parish priest, preferring to turn his present 'ecclesial community' into a parish and ignoring the greater 'ecclesiastical area'.

In my more lucid moments, I feel a certain affinity with his predicament. Despite the spiritual heights to which I theoretically aspire, in practice I retain unhappy memories of a system that had more to do with the preservation of power and control than the effective preaching of God's word. Donald Nicoll writes that the more balanced and reliable people are craftsmen, workers who by virtue of their occupation assume responsibility for their own work and cannot blame other people for their failures and imperfections. Priesting is a craft too, and keeping curates in a state of arrested adolescence, while it has much to commend it, encourages irresponsibility and promotes inefficiency. Like Arthur Miller's Willie Loman,

'Attention, attention must be finally paid to such a person.'

At the same time, like marriage, every relationship between *parochus et curatus* is not made in heaven. We journey on life's pilgrimage with different accoutrements and the varied possibilities and limitations that life thrusts on us. Differences of ages, temperament, even interest, can strain the personal resources of clerical twosomes and cause no small amount of stress and dissension. Unshared enthusiasms (for golf or the liturgy), a certain perceived lethargy (home visitation, or, more seriously, the collection of dues), clerical popularity contests (thinly disguised as community projects) and the endless personal rivalries that are the result of over-priesting areas of dwindling population, can cause rifts in the quiet tenor of clerical and parish life. Out of the most unpromising circumstances, even lifelong feuds can be harvested.

Parochi et curati are now quite different species, speak different languages, own different theologies and have different perceptions of duty, responsibility, even of Church. On the one side, there is the traditional deference to the accumulated wisdom of the past, couched in official statements, to directives that come with episcopal approval or a Vatican letterhead; a hunger for order, ritual, formality and ecclesiastical protocol; a preoccupation with linking current practice to the tradition of the Church, a growing respect for the memory of Pius XII. On the other side, there is the pre-eminence of personal experience; an acute sense of the 'signs of the times'; a distrust of what is perceived as Roman bureaucracy and centralised administration; a distaste for the pomp and triumphalism that others regard as propriety and convention; a fascination with interpreting the truths of faith in the currency of our times, and who is Pius XII?

For PP and CC, it is my experience that the principal constraint on the number of disagreements is the comparative rarity of encounters. Unfortunately, that amenable truth is not, as the canon lawyer might say, always spontaneously achievable. I remember a bit of tetchiness about the bishop wanting one of us to go on a renewal course (we tossed, I won and he had to go); a remark passed about PPs who expected bishops to send them not curates but ordained spaniels; a discussion on presence in the liturgy that contained the (I thought) pointed suggestion that acceptable demeanour in sitting on the President's chair in the sanctuary didn't necessarily entail a masterful impression of a man milking a cow; a question about whether all non-essential parish expenditure had to be perceived as a form of moral turpitude; and, not least, a quotation from the American Catholic novelist, J. F. Power, suggesting that a curate was a mouse training to be a rat!

There are other cultivated eccentricities too: a disconcerting disinterest in bingo and golf; a penchant in conversation for using sentences so labyrinthine and words so polysyllabic that he had at intervals to pause for deep breaths; a beautiful singing voice with which he gave widely admired displays of what he called 'his four-octave vocal dynamics'; a distressing popularity with the people; a fetish for the word 'community'; a tendency to recreate with the laity in the local public house; a habit of demanding that every one call him Derek; and a doubtful habit of telling risque jokes at weddings and kissing the nuns at Christmas. Which latter custom places him in the same school of protocol as an American curate (or what our confrères on the wrong side of the Atlantic call an 'associate pastor') who comes each year to Kilmacshalgan to visit his Irish cousins. Once he arrives, the local PP immediately goes on holidays. The sign of peace alone, the PP claims, could be regarded as sufficient grounds for reconsecrating the church.

A confrère, the diocesan wag, describes his relationship with his PP as being 'based on mutual understanding. He thinks I'm for the birds and I think he's cuckoo!' Not every association achieves such profound rapport, but many strive mightily for it. A curate, whose PP was inordinately conscious of the dizzy heights to which he had risen in the local church, had occasion to communicate with him by letter in their scattered, out-of-the-way parish. The curate's persistence in addressing the letters to 'Rev. Father' rather than 'Venerable Archdeacon' was held to be responsible for his elder confrère becoming almost a schizophrenic, the unfortunate postman a nervous wreck – in that, like a latter-day Amalekite, he was blamed in this case not so much for the content of the message as the address on the envelope – and the curate's own happy transfer to a more fertile vineyard. And there is the authoritative testimony of the PP, who, after years expending energy in multifarious directions and accumulating neither great sanctity nor wealth, came to the conclusion that the ideal parish was one which had no hall, no school, no church and, especially, no curate.

Thrown together by time, circumstance and more than a little faith, PP and CC centre, hopefully in something approaching unison, on the worship, wisdom and identity of their people. Ships in the night, schooners maybe, battleships occasionally, voyagers of discovery, pilgrims of faith. At best often an uneasy alliance under a heavy weight of varying perceptions and perspectives. The one pining for the death of innocence, the other for the demise of concupiscence; one knowing how to fundraise to good effect, the other where the anthems to the BVM are in the breviary. The one rebuilding his golf-swing; the other his spiritual life; the one enthusing about Vatican II; the other eating All-Bran every morning and worrying about piles; the mesmeric agitation of the activist, the more prudent and lethargic philosophy of *festina lente*. All clerical life is there.

VIII   Disturbing the peace

In an unaccustomed fit of modesty, let me declaim, dear reader, an essential truth. Lisnagoola is not the centre of the universe. If the truth were told, it isn't, despite my pretensions, the most significant of pastorates. It is, in effect analogically, a second-cousin once removed of the gulag of the diocese.

The word 'gulag' has a certain appropriateness to it , shades of Sakharov and the possibility of a triumphant return to 'Moscow', and I use it advisedly. I have had to endure not seldom in clerical conversation an unpauline comparison of my native diocese to the human body and, to complete the analogy, my *Cura Animarum* compared to one of the least impressive parts of the human anatomy. But I let it pass. *Sorte sua contentus.*

For one thing, Lisnagoola is, and I have failed to find a less innocuous word, backward. God has thankfully conceded through the geographical features of the area to limit, in so far as God can, physical access to the place. Civilisation, or what passes for it hereabouts, is half-a-lifetime away, a not inconsiderable boon in that it both justifies the possession of a car considerably above the clerical ante, and it dissuades my precedessors from returning for every liturgical cockfight. We gratefully record the non-existence of that sociological perennial of late twentieth-century culture, the video rental shop, or that culinary oxymoron which Americans call 'fast-food'. We are in a sense the Irish equivalent of the Amish, and if it snows we might as well be in Siberia.

For all of which, once I got over the shock I am, *per Deum et episcopum*, suitably and irredeemably grateful. Even though superficially all I survey may be less than it might be, I am nonetheless monarch of it, a not inconsiderable *quid pro quo*. There is also the consideration that, thanks to recurring emigration, the population has been suitably devastated. For all its social consequences, it has left me in the ideal pastoral situation of having little or nothing to do.

Another boon is its relative impenetrability to outside influences. In the last general election, for instance, it was discovered that, when the appropriate ballot-box was opened and the tallymen did their count, someone had actually voted Labour, an unprecedented display of political independence ultimately traced to an erstwhile student of a third-level institution. This act of political outrage generated the communal reaction 'Wouldn't you think he'd know what side his bread was buttered on?' Lisnagoola, in nineteenth century terms, would be Cullen as distinct from Newman country, with perhaps a touch of McHale thrown in before his demotion to Tuam. The ultramontane ethic is alive and well and resting nicely in Lisnagoola, thank you very much.

Indeed, since my unexpected arrival here, I have often contemplated recording in book-form, in hardback naturally, the essentials of a benign pastorate, *à la* Lisnagoola. I could call it something like *The Contentment Factor*. This is not to be confused with the kind of medical paperback which seeks to explain exceptions to our much-vaunted Hipprocratic wisdom: why moderate drinkers live longer than Pioneers, why people who enjoy their food live longer than those who diet obsessively or, devastatingly, why men who have a partner live longer than those who are single (*L'Osservatore Romano* and other Vatican papers, please copy). *Quoad potero perferam*.

No, my magnum opus would propose the following:

(i) the adoption of the *festina lente* philosophy as an appropriate ethos for the modern Church.

(ii) the need in this cyclical culture to avoid, or at least minimalise, change of any kind on the basis that today's fashion, like time-ravaged bell-bottomed trousers at clerical golf outings, are ultimately derivative of yesterday's wisdom.

(iii) the proposal that non-activism is not just a healthy antidote to the bustle of modern life but a necessary prelude to reflection, and

(iv) the over-riding principle that the best solution to every problem is to pray about it.

The main benefit of this approach, the result of distilled reflection on the pastoral scene for almost half a century, is that it leaves the pastor of souls with more or less nothing to do.

My intention would be to propose humble Lisnagoola as a model. I could, in the wake of a veritable host of liturgical and other gurus, devise 'a programme' for eliciting this pastoral panacea, even in the most unlikely circumstances. I could even take to the lecture circuit, and avail of all those episcopal invitations to fill gaps innocuously in conferences, 'to do good' and end up, like so many others, doing very well indeed.

All of that was before Lisnagoola's tranquillity, and my plans, were somewhat disturbed by the arrival of Daphne. A native of the parish, her return after a lengthy sojourn in Tennessee was perceived by her as an opportunity to visit the benefits of her mainly feminist wisdom on the good people of Lisnagoola and, worse still, on me. How unlovely on the mountains of Lisnagoola was this good news, communicated to me by her unsuspecting mother at our bi-annual meeting of the Legion of Mary. Unlike Teresa of Avila, Daphne doesn't believe that God strolls amid the pots and pans. Rather, she herself feels called among the cruets and chalices. It is a task, nay a vocation, to which she brings a deadly seriousness and while humour has just about squeezed its way into her lexicon, irony is a foreign body. Drawing on her wide experience of priestless parishes somewhere to the south-east of Talahassee Bridge, and disconcertingly quoting verbatim long passages from some relatively recent Papal document called *Christifideles Laici*, she presented a ten-point plan for dragging Lisnagoola, as she put it, 'into the mainstream of Church life'. It was as follows:

(i) the immediate abolition of sexist language in the liturgy and the establishment of a 'watchdog' committee to monitor progress

(ii) calling God 'he' subtly reinforced the notion of male superiority and should be discontinued forthwith

(iii) the immediate introduction of altar girls, a trivial matter in itself but apparently of symbolic significance

(iv) the washing of women's feet on Holy Thursday Night and, I suspect, the licking of their boots for the rest of the year

(v) the involvement of women in decision-making at all levels of the parish

(vi) an equal representation of women on the Parish Council, the Liturgy Group, the Ushers' Committee, the Lectors' Panel and an equal representation of men on the Cleaners' List. 'Gender Equity', I think, was the phrase she used.

(vii) resources to be made available from parish funds for women's studies, with a view to developing a full-time female ministry in the parish, a position for which Daphne declared herself available

(viii) a renewal course of at least six months' duration for my good self and, on my return, a commitment that the women of the parish be involved in my continuing formation

(ix) help, the nature of which was not thankfully specified, with any hurt I myself might have experienced in my efforts to integrate my sexuality, a hurt which I myself might at present be denying or avoiding with defence mechanisms like golf or bingo

(x) a complete refurbishment of the liturgical wardrobe.

My enthusiasm for her agenda was tempered somewhat by the knowledge that of the committees she intended to reform, not all of them in fact existed and some I'd never heard of. I suggested *moribus antiquis* that we should pray about it – a propostion which she at first received with a curiously muted fervour but soon transmogrified into a proposal for what seemed like a feminist liturgical extravaganza. I suggested that, as liturgy could easily become a sublimation of the work ethic, perhaps we could compromise on a Holy Hour during Lent. She found my theory 'interesting'. I found it enigmatic to the point of meaninglessness, but it served its purpose. Though not so with the redoubtable Fr Derek, my curate by the grace of God and the perversion the bishop.

A visit from a curate is, like buttermilk, not quite what it used to be. A quiet tipple on a cold winter's evening, a chance to reminisce over the doughty past with a captive and, for the most part, attentive audience, a bit of advice on how to deal with some ticklish pastoral problem. That sort of thing. *Quanta qualis errant illa sabbata.*

The agenda now is more contentious, the approach more adversarial, the style inquisitorial. A sorting out of areas of responsibilities, an unsolicited instruction in Eucharistic theology when Quarantore comes around, a conversation of such ambiguous vacuity that later on it will be alluded to as the green light for some undreamt of liturgical delinquency.

Fr Derek alluded to one such conversation. It was for him a memorable breakthrough in that I had apparently conceded that a sharp campaign to stretch 'the concept of ministry in the liturgical arena' was a priority for Lisnagoola.

I myself had no precise recollection of this exchange, though on reflection it may well have been in the wake of one of those recently mooted seminars which we are prevailed upon to attend irregularly. We come, in truth, not to seek guidance or wisdom but out of loyalty, or is it duty, or the sheer boredom of drizzly afternoons? I have accordingly, over the years, developed a certain bemused restraint at the flights of fancy to which experts are sometimes subject, and I pride myself on my natural ability for keeping things in perspective. The fact that this approach admirably coincides with my personal *festina lente* philosophy of life is a bonus which, in my declining years, I unambiguously cherish. Derek, in a fit of pique, or was it just contrived exasperation, recently enquired whether I had heard of the new support group called Parish Priests Anonymous? Apparently it works on the principle that if any PP is tempted to change anything, the group will immediately gather to dissuade him.

The Synod document is a case in point. *Christifideles Laici*, 'the lay faithful' for the benefit of those who have not as yet celebrated their silver jubilees, makes several telling points about involving lay people in the Church 'with a sense of urgency'. Derek arrived one evening to present me with a copy and I felt the least I

might do was actually read it. It was a slim volume in an appropriately red cover, but, in true Vatican style, practically impenetrable.

Indeed it is, in universal form, redolent of my conversations
with Derek. Later on it will be quoted to sustain quite opposing
positions; it is subject to quite unnecessary wadding in the form
of quotations from other similar documents, and it is written in
the kind of prose which, after a maximum of two and a half
pages, defeats the most persistent or even masochistic of readers.
It is a form of communication that apparently endeavours to disguise whatever message it strives to transmit. It takes only a
nodding acquaintance with the excesses of Church history to
conclude that unfortunates have been toasted over flames for a
lot less.

Derek, it transpires, like the rest of the Irish Church, has not
actually read the document itself, but has devoured several
summaries of its content. He is particularly taken with that
phrase 'a sense of urgency' which pops up *passim*, and has mis-
guidedly concluded that this suggests that we should actually
do something. I try to dissuade him of this unperceptive conclusion. Documents like this, I tell him, are simply expressions of an
ideal. They are not intended to be taken literally. They are no
more than useful indicators of the direction in which the Church
may, after a century or two, actually move. The varied 'models
of Church' which out-of-work theologians drum up to try and
revive a falling market – have flip-chart, will travel – offer, I suggest to Derek, little more than partial insights into the mind of
the Church. The pyramid model and the circular model, which
Derek loves to draw on his flip-chart, have their own truth but
the more perceptive model is that of the barque of Peter going
around in concentric circles. The strength of tradition, the history
of the Church, the fallibility of human nature, and so on, necessitate a certain prudence in our response.

Unhappily, Derek dismisses that circumspect approach. Prudence,
he says, is one of the minor virtues. And even though in the en-
suing discussion, which teeters on the brink of becoming a row, I
marshall all the best arguments, appeal to the authority of tradi-

tion and make several telling points, Derek, distressingly seems to interpret all this caution, perspicacity and discretion as a roundabout way of making a virtue of inactivity.

The antidote to all this philosophical inertia, he suggests, is a sustained effort to expand or develop varied liturgical ministries. Despite all my reservations about the apparent reluctance of the laity to come forward, or the inappropriateness of this time of year for such novelties, or the need to ponder for several months, if not years, a suitably felicitous strategy for such a departure from current practice, it all seemed to no avail. Worse still, I could see in my mind's eye the distinctly uninviting prospect of meetings multiplying themselves rabbit-like into a series of a series. It was, after all, going to be a long and difficult winter.

Fr Derek, as is his way, suggested – with a firmness that belied his reputation for gentleness when dealing with laity of the junior sex – that he would train readers, instruct lay ministers of the Eucharist, teach a representative selection how to compose bidding prayers, and draw up a rota of teenagers to deliver them. I, on the other hand, was to devote my considerable personal talents and organisational flair to training altar-boys. In a previous altercation, the possibility of initiating altar-girls had been ruled out. Ploughing approved furrows is one thing; opening new ones is quite another. *Laudator temporis acti.*

The inevitable corollary to that even distribution of responsibilities was that each of us would indicate active support for the other. From past experience I realised that 'active support' could be a distressingly moveable feast.

In my innocence, I fondly imagined that putting a bit of a shape on the altar-boys would be a fairly innocuous exercise. It was, however, a prospect I didn't relish. For one thing, I'm distinctly allergic to these juvenile liturgical functionaries. For another, it is my belief that as the miracle of electric power has tendered candles redundant, the new liturgy has in effect created the same admirable condition vis-a-vis altar-boys. For which happy reason they are now a threatened liturgical species.

My approach, accordingly, was to diminish their status as much as possible and to relegate them to the liturgical fringe. Unfortunately this approach of 'say nothing, do nothing, touch nothing' was unacceptable to my perversely inflexible colleague. For someone who is so low Church as to be distinctly sepulchral, Derek has a great fondness for the liturgical excesses of High Churchism. Bells are not for jingling but for pealing, incense not for casting a subtle hum on the air but for wafting in great clouds into the rafters, holy water is not for sprinkling but for drenching unsuspecting parishioners.

Altar-boys are, therefore, encouraged to keep their busy fingers in every liturgical pie. New outfits, with hoods and cinctures attached, were purchased at quite ridiculous expense and the whole cohort took on the appearance of miniature versions of the Knights of the Holy Sepulchre. Hours on end were spent instructing ten-year-olds with suspect coordination the complicated business of using the thurible. Young lads of limited intelligence were expected to deal with a series of complicated manoeuvres, the logistics of which they couldn't possibly master and the purpose of which I couldn't quite fathom. How many carpets would be destroyed with candlegrease, how many thuribles effortlessly and interminably entangled, how many tempers lost, I could only wonder.

Even though I showed a conspicuous lack of enthusiasm for the whole business, it did nothing to temper Derek's penchant for complicated movement, excessive attention to liturgical norms and interminable processions. He himself evinced a peculiar inability to recognise the definitive giddiness of our young horrors and the predictable fallout in terms of confusion, tension and possible loss of life.

I could visualise myself on Palm Sunday, or in the procession to the altar of repose on Maundy Thursday, or carrying the baby Jesus to the crib on Christmas night, a loping cadaverous figure, a liturgical Gulliver surrounded by a clutch of begowned Lilliputians, emanating an intensity of solemn foolishness as I struggled vainly to keep rein on my charges, like a demented shepherd without his faithful dog. I could forsee an endless series of rehearsals to minimise the predictable anarchy. And above all I could see my own particular gaggle of Mass-servers lighting the candles at the wrong time on Holy Saturday night, disappearing out the front door of the church with crucifix and candles instead of leading the offertory procession, arriving with thurible and incense during the consecration, and generally behaving in that enthusiastically incompetent way of children that delights parents and infuriates other more emotionally discriminating members of the human race.

Timor reverencialis, that mixture of fear and reverence, so much part of the aura surrounding the *parochus* in the past, no longer acts as a deterrent on the excesses of altar boys. Or maybe it is just that, in my declining years, I am becoming progressively more reluctant to play a part in a drama produced by someone else … feminist, clerical iconoclast, anyone.

IX Horses for courses

Summer in Lisnagoola is, in the main, gratifyingly uneventful. There is, in rural parts, a pastoral wisdom that is at once consoling and pertinent. With schools closed, the sun shining – well, at least occasionally – work in field and farm to be attended to, holiday-makers to welcome, there is a perceptible decline – if that is possible – in the workload of the rural pastor. Our city confrères may find this difficult to imagine, but truth to tell, in summertime in rural parts we more or less close down the shop.

It's a sensible course. It allows the people of God a temporary respite from our sometimes fussy ministrations, it's off-season for bingo, and it permits hard-pressed pastors an opportunity to unwind after the stresses and the strains of a busy year.

Consequently, to institutionalise this pastoral *sos*, two series of alternate distractions fill the vacuum and help while away the summer: the first and more important, a series of diocesan and other golf competitions culminating in the prestigious Killala Open in Enniscrone, and the second, such a multiplicity of worthy courses that every possible interest, indeed obsession, is more than adequately catered for.

What's more, the two alternatives are known to dovetail with remarkable ingenuity in that a mid-week break in Ballybunion or Lahinch and a series of lectures in Marianella or Milltown Park on 'The Arian Heresy in the Fourth Century' can both be covered by a terse, businesslike notice in the parish bulletin, 'Father will be away on a course until Friday'.

The old adage 'If a priest plays golf and is good to his mother, he won't go far wrong' is curiously no longer widely quoted, but it's surely a wellspring of clerical wisdom. Golf, whatever about mothers, makes a substantial contribution to a wholesome clerical life in that it's so physically demanding that it helps us to sleep, so obsessive that it distracts from unhealthy phobias about celibacy or involving laity in the Church, and it gives us something to do on holidays besides contemplating the futility of life.

As well as that, it allows for a legitimate form of fantasising, in that even the most pathetic exponent can convince himself that quite unachievable, even incomprehensible levels of performance may not in fact be beyond him, or worse still her. Those of us whose lives are in the main unremarkable, but who harbour warranted suspicions that behind our unpromising exteriors are unpromising interiors, can sometimes, from the flimsiest of evidence on the golf course, convince ourselves that such may not be the case. It is only of course because of the cruellest luck on the greens, or the lunatic placement of sand-bunkers by the insufferable idiot who designed the course, or the lumbar twinges that prevent the silkiest of swings, or an unhappy childhood, or too little affirmation from one's PP or worse still one's curate, or whatever litany of excuses golfers invent to explain their inadequacies, that is inhibiting the emergence of a quite exceptional golfing talent. The great charm of golf is that, on occasion, unremarkable golfers can do remarkable things. As well as that, like jogging, golf has other things going for it; you get exercise and fresh air, it can be intensely pleasurable, and most of the time it's not sinful.

So, complete with Church and General hold-all, C & G umbrella, C & G golf balls, C & G tees, and other complimentary artefacts collected over the years from an insurance company that at every opportunity imprints blue and red birds on the clerical subconcious, I became practically a full-time member of the diocesan golfing circuit.

In fact, my outings, particularly in the balmy days of late June and early July, are so numerous that I feel it incumbent on me to retain the expedient ambiguity of the phrase 'away on a course'.

What I felt I needed was something less demanding than listen-ing to some enthusiastic academic working himself, or worse still herself, into an emotional state over some peripheral issue like adult catechesis, or some of those awful 'process-people' breaking up every innocuous gathering into 'groups'. What really suited my requirement was something light and bubbly, a modern cocktail that would leave the palate dry but would en-hance my reputation for psazz, panache and seriousness of mind.

The list is gratifyingly endless. Gort Mhuire, Marianella, Tallaght, Maynooth – the latter to be avoided at all costs or you could find yourself organising yet another diocesan collection for yet another Japanese fountain. Back to poor Viola in *Twelfth Night* again: 'I am all the daughters of my father's house', 'and all the brothers too.' I think I know how she felt. A full-time sem-inar freak could indeed eventually learn to be all things to all men, as well as to a reasonable phalanx of women. The problem was that, from glancing curiously through the 'Gazette' page – it goes to show you, you never know when you might need *Intercom* – I quickly came to the conclusion that I couldn't really understand what they meant. Titles like Reflexology, Holism, Dreams Workshop, Myers-Briggs, Chinese Medicine, the Enneagram and so on, danced enigmatically before my eyes. What did they mean? Was there a hidden agenda that I'd missed out on after all those years? And nothing on The Third Way?

I took advice from a nun who has something of a reputation as a course-freak. What would she recommend? I knew by her reac-tion that she was glad to help. After twenty-five years offering unsolicited advice to any and every member of the clergy who had the misfortune to bump into her, this prospect was too good to miss. A phone call metamorphosed itself into a meeting. Life is like that. The ability to say simple things in a short space of time is progressively disappearing from civilised congress. 'What about the Dreams Workshop?' she enquired, adding enigmatically, 'at your stage in life'. It sounded too much like an occasion of sin so I passed it off. What about Reflexology? What was it? A way of manipulating the pressure points on the soles of your feet to suss out physical ailments? And who would do it when I'd come home? The housekeeper? And what would the

bishop say if he found out? I tried to steer her clear of reflexology, not just because I found it difficult to envisage myself lying
on my back with my unstockinged feet in the air and having
them scratched by some well-meaning nun, but I was afraid
that, if I didn't divert my advisor from the medical arena, I'd
never get her out of the house. I intimated that, for whatever
years God left me, I'd prefer to stay with conventional medicine.
That was fine with her, she graciously conceded, but had I heard
that a confrère of mine recently had a malfunction of the genito-
urinary system diagnosed by a Reflexology colleague of her own?

No doubt all of this is second nature to our urban confrères but
it's big news in this part of the world. And as she spoke, it reminded me vaguely of the enthusiast in Swift's *Lapute* who
spent eight years busily trying to extract sunbeams from cucum-
bers. For one thing, I felt it somehow wasn't me but, worse still,
it had definite overtones of antisocial behaviour if not good old-
fashioned sin.

As delicately as I could, I tried to divert her from what seemed a
plethora of medical neuroses given mock status by gatherings of
like-minded eccentrics, and I indicated – gently, I hope – my
reluctance to join such a group.

The modern conference, as David Lodge mischievously points
out in *Small World*, resembles the pilgrimage of medieval
Christendom in that it allows the participants to indulge themselves in all kinds of pleasures and diversions while appearing
to be austerely bent on self-improvement. The few penitential
exercises involved, like listening to the ponderous delivery of
dull papers and wearing clerical garb on the journey there and
back, are a small price to pay for a week spent in some hazy
haven of bucolic bliss, meeting distinguished theologians, form-
ing new and interesting friendships, visiting the theatre, sampling the gastronomic oblations of gourmet restaurants, and
eventually returning home with an enhanced reputation for
seriousness of mind.

With so many gifted people pushing their disciplines to such
lengths, I felt cheered in my own intention to indulge in a bit of

reactionary frivolity. I toyed momentarily with the possibility of attending a conference on 'New Developments in Human Reproduction: Vision and Choices', a subject sufficiently topical to generate a certain intellectual curiosity and sufficiently abstruse to pander to my academic pretensions. Lady Warnock might very well be able to throw some light on her Report, but the spectre of 'professionals in medicine, law, social science, ethics and theology' discussing it at great length was too much to cope with on a 'soft' Lisnagoola day. The fact that no one – except the Baroness herself and two Irish moral theologians – understands the subject sufficiently to discuss it with any advantage, plus the memory of years of eaves-dropping on the emotional biology of that post-prandial radio programme *Liveline*, caused me to give it a miss. One down and one hundred and one to go.

My eye lit on a 'Senior Catechetics Course'. After years of mediocre wanderings through *The Moral Life*, I decided against even a passing visit to the scenes of my past crimes. Unfond memories of a previous catechetics binge, which involved mostly lying on the broad of my back in a large room with about thirty other mesmerised participants being urged on by some crazed, polo-necked religious to relax, relax, relax, tempered the fading remnants of my enthusiasm. Catechetics courses, in my experience, tend to consist mainly of pooled frustration. Like gardening, the reality never quite matches the vision.

After dawdling for a while with 'Desert Spirituality', I drew another blank on the grounds that what I really needed was a break from the Lisnagoola 'Desert', and anyway a week would scarcely provide the increasingly fashionable 'Genesee' experience *à la* Henri Nouwen. A seminar on 'Living Theology', as distinct presumably from Dying Theology, was likewise dismissed, conscious as I am in my declining years both of my increasing inability to question my own assumptions and the growing need to fight the quiet battle of faith. The prospect of all that enthusiasm seemed about as welcome as a dead mouse in a loaf of bread.

Eventually I opted for a course on Liturgical Music. Not blessed with the slightest indication of musical or singing ability, it was like someone with a medical history of pyromania behind him applying for a position in a match factory. In the event, talent was an unnecessary prerequisite: all that was needed was money. A confrère told me I was 'wasting my time', that peculiarly Irish form of clerical encouragement, but it was nonetheless a practical concern and it promised a certain variety.

My announcement on Sunday that I would be away on a course was received with customary disinterest. I quickly added that it had to do with liturgical music, in case they might wonder whether the course in question might be Royal Dublin or Lahinch. My fears were groundless. The stolid indifference of my people sometimes discourages, but then again liturgical music is hardly a pressing concern. Their cares tend to be more basic and mine, no doubt, evidence of an eerie, idiosyncratic world often quite beyond their ken.

On the course itself, to my surprise, the clergy comprised only a tiny minority of the participants, most involved in organisation, a few high-powered musicians, and one tone-deaf bystander from Lisnagoola. The rest were young or nuns or, very occasionally, both. The young, clearly in the majority, were loud, hairy and guitar-playing. Most were attired in rampant denim and sequinned bomber jackets, and one distinguished-looking youth sported jagged hair styles with each spike a separate colour of the rainbow. It struck me that if some of the more psychedelic participants turned up in Lisnagoola on a Sunday morning we'd hardly let them inside the church, not to speak of leading the choir. It says something, probably about Lisnagoola.

The nuns were more restrained, most of them being veterans of an extraordinary variety of courses, most of which seemed to have to do with personality development and spiritual growth. Phrases like 'finding yourself' and 'making space' and 'getting inside' and 'staying with the question' peppered the conversation. Most discarded their veils as being a barrier to real communication, others wore ordinary clothes and a few were, for all the world, like refugees from *Upstairs, Downstairs*.

The formal proceedings were kept to a minimum. Lectures were short, in the morning, and available in photocopied form if you happened to sleep in, which for different reasons most of the participants contrived to do. Workshops constituted the main thrust of a conference, on Folk Music, Choral Singing, Gregorian Chant, Taizé Music, Effective Reading of the Scriptures and, finally and mysteriously, Motivation.

Participants were expected to circulate, which meant in effect rambling around from one group to another. This arrangement suited me admirably, in that passing encounter is always less exacting than permanent commitment. The Folk Group Session was packed, youths mainly, of all shapes and sizes, clinging to the rafters, strumming countless guitars and participating in what looked vaguely like a spontaneous gesticulation competition. Confusion reigned supreme. In the Choral Session order was the order of the day. Comprised mainly of nuns singing as sweetly as only nuns can, I escaped after learning a new word 'Descants'. In the Gregorian Group the key word was gloom. A few aged participants exchanged depressions and a well worn copy of a thick black hymnal, bearing the legend *Liber Usualis*, sat symbolically on a low table. From time to time, an Archdeacon would lay his hand lovingly on the book and reminise about the good old days. The Taizé Group was all about atmosphere and was conducted in shuttered darkness, broken by votive lights randomly placed around a small room. Participants were encouraged to sit on tiny prayer stools, an exercise which involved elaborate anatomical contortions. The possibility of doing oneself damage in the process couldn't be ruled out, but a greater worry was that some aged nun might suddenly go up in flames. The Scripture Reading session was conducted by an earnest young man who both knew how to read and was no stranger to the Scriptures. And, finally, the 'Motivation' session was confined to priests, who exchanged case histories about how to generate enthusiasm for liturgical music or, in some cases, about how to dampen it down.

The course concluded with the inevitable party, cheese and white wine, much back-slapping and hearty bonhomie, a lot of smiling and waving and occasionally rising on the balls of one's feet to get a glimpse of the visiting celebrities: theologians whose reputation had deteriorated into fame, and bishops whose fame was in danger of developing into reputation. It was all quite enjoyable, apart from an intolerably tedious conversation with an ageing radical who gave short sermonettes on dialectical materialism and the dictatorship of the proletariat, and a semi-distraught nun who kept repeating 'conscientisation' and holding forth on the reality of sin and the need to be what she called 'a free spirit'. You can, as the saying goes, get too much of a good thing.

The real test of this freeing spirit – or course-freak, depending on how you look at it – is to submit yourself, not to a detached nod in the direction of some indifferent discipline, but to the misery of self-examination.

X A voyage
around the Enneagram

There comes a stage in life when clerical gentlemen, of similar vintage to myself, experience what the experts call 'a sense of dislocation'. It is akin to the feeling that life is not so much passing by as disappearing over the horizon, that almost after a lifetime of struggling in whatever corner of God's vineyard we are either blessed or afflicted with, we end up with the imprecise feeling that we are playing a part in a play written by someone else. 'Is this all there is?' we hear ourselves ask.

This pickle is not to be confused with the kind of angst that asphyxiates precocious little seagulls with unlikely names like Jonathan Livingstone, or the congenital restlessness of the human spirit that is too cosily dismissed by Augustine's natty aphorism. Nor is it to be confused with 'Burnout', which latter condition invariably afflicts those who have something to do.

Perhaps it can best be described as a form of philosophical vertigo and nature contrives a variety of coping mechanisms. Some confrères develop an interest in physical activity and purchase the kind of multicoloured tracksuit that looks admirable on lithe athletes or on those artificially slender extra-terrestrials in television advertisements for Special K breakfasts, but can appear catastrophic on figures usually disguised by the gratifying fullness of alb and chasuble. The effect can be unintentionally comic on those who, like a load in a wheelbarrow, have most of their assets in front of them.

Others take a year off to find themselves and usually disappear altogether. Others again lapse into what they imagine is a dignified form of terminal cynicism. Still others try to recapture the remnants of whatever academic dream drifts into consciousness from an uneasy past and confirms the unwarranted contention that their considerable gifts are not being properly used, for the glory of God, of course, in this neck of the woods. Invariable, what follows is either a course brushing up on medieval Italian in order to read Dante in the original, or a sufficient knowledge of modern literary theory to enable them to explain symbiotics at cheese and wine parties, or immersing themselves in that fashionable pessimism that demands the ability to quote undigested lumps of Kierkegaard. And people like myself, congenitally addicted to exploring the curious avenues and byways of human behaviour, and innumerable cul-de-sacs as well, do the Enneagram.

A certain trepidation, if the truth were told, attended the journey. The expert, to whose tutelage I was to submit my delicate person for most of a week, was a sister, not a nun, as she graciously pointed out to me by way of sermonette, who had a reputation as something of a feminist. I am, let me admit, allergic to feminist nuns, having witnessed at first hand over the years the convent revolution. God be with the days when judicious nuns drew from their fat missals the frayed prayer:

I'll go where you want me to go, dear Lord,
Over mountains or valleys or sea.
I'll say what you want me to say, dear Lord,
I'll be what you want me to be.

No doubt the modern version runs something like this:

I'll go where I want to go, dear Lord,
To party or function or tea.
I'll say whatever I want to say,
I'll be wherever I'll be.

And have you noticed those increasingly truculent nuns who, in an effort to undo the perceived damage to the male clerical psyche by attentive if not doting nuns in the past, feel it incumbent on them not to compromise their feminist credentials by even passing the salt?

From my cursory knowledge of what the Enneagram entailed, I

was aware that such a venture into the uncharted waters of the inner life could involve jettisoning a plethora of subtle rationalisations lovingly constructed over the decades to make life a bit more tolerable. Human kind, Eliot said, can't bear much reality, and, to add to the discomfort, someone reminded me of Virginia Woolf's dismissal of Joyce's *Ulysses* as akin to a queasy undergraduate scratching his spots, which by association did very little for my belated cruise into the choppy waters of self-examination. And there was too, I realised, the danger, with all this unremitting introspection, of forgetting the real world of living and partly living.

The Enneagram, for the unitiated, is a way of identifying and, worse still, admitting the prevailing compulsions of nine basic personality types. Classical scholars who prefer to use terms like *fissure in ano* to explain at station-breakfasts the reason for tomorrow's haemorrhoidal visit to a Dublin proactologist, will no doubt understand the derivation. What follows, by way of public service, is very much a beginner's guide.

Ones are people who feel a compulsion to be perfect. They love rules, are always on time and work hard. For obvious reasons, few of them are clergy. *Ones* have a devastating tendency to make mountains out of molehills. Curates who tend to make molehills out of mountains, are rarely *Ones*.

Twos tend to be warm, helpful and sensitive. Older nuns tend to be *Twos*, and *Twos*, whatever about older nuns, are prone to infatuation and, under stress, to flattery and manipulation. Nuns in general … on second thoughts, better not.

Threes are busy, competitive, enthusiastic and energised people who feed off success but fail to acknowledge the contribution of others to that success. Builders of churches and hewers of wood?

Fours are special, unique, even precious. Every event is a drama in the making and the only inexhaustible source of interest is oneself. They can have a phenomenal sense of their own importance and believe no one can experience things quite like they can. I sometimes wonder how many bishops are *Fours*.

Fives are observers rather than participants. They stand aside and analyse. NCPI delegates, possibly? *Fives* collect information and pursue knowledge rather than feelings, and are often to be found in Marriage Tribunals.

Sixes are indecisive because they see all the snags. PPs? They tend to be loyal and obedient: PPs under the age of retirement? *Sixes* can border on the scattered. One notorious *Six* mislaid several Trócaire boxes which were discovered in the boot of his car by the garage after he had changed it.

Sevens are hyper-active, future-oriented, pain-avoiders who like to be in the middle of the stage with the spotlight shining directly on them. They tend to be cheerful and optimistic, but like Tolstoy's Sisters tend to live in a world of essentially unrealised expectations. Curates on the verge of parishes? Performers in Holy Shows?

Eights are aggressive, intimidatory, confrontational, attention-seekers who bulldoze their way through others and who deal in possessiveness and submission. In the good old days, *Eights* were almost always bishops, were occasionally PPs, and are now progressively an unhappily unthreatened species of curate.

And then there are *Nines*, among whose number my feminist friend unerringly and unsurprisingly placed me. The *Nine* is easy-going, inactive, avoids conflict, values harmony and is generally a black and white, if not colourless, individual.

Before my Enneagram (BME), I used to imagine fondly that I had developed my humility to a tolerable degree, in fact I took a certain pride in doing so, but after my Enneagram (AME), I discovered that in fact my self-esteem was underdeveloped. BME I felt I had the ability to balance the pros and cons of a particular issue, but AME I discovered I was prone to indecision. BME I regarded myself as, I think the Americanism is, 'laid back', but AME I realised that the *festina lente* philosophy I had developed so assiduously was in effect a form of indolence.

My pastoral policy based on Martin Heidegger's concept of 'active waiting', while it presented to the initiated as a form of non-

activity, was uncovered as a conspiracy to remain out of the
limelight in case someone might ask me to do something. The
assembled illuminati nodded sagely and agreed that the unlikely
set of circumstances I was waiting to converge so that I could
'get stuck into the parish' were not just possibly improbable, but
probably impossible, and were in effect a subtle disguise for a
benign form of lethargy.

My interest in *Glenroe*, *Neighbours* and *Coronation Street* was interpreted as a compensatory emotional attachment to the television; my instinctive embracing of a policy of 'Why stand if you
can sit down – why sit if you can lie down?' was evidence of a
debilitating torpor; my unbroken sleep pattern was indicative of
an unhealthy taciturnity; my partiality for good food, a few
games of golf a week and collecting Grecian artefacts was, I was
told, compelling evidence that I was a *Nine*.

It isn't easy, this post-enneagrammatic life. Words like 'challenge', 'freedom' and 'healing' have a curious habit of sounding
better in Dublin than they do when I get back to Lisnagoola. The
Enneagram people may well be the new secular clergy but, in
my declining years, can I really bear that much reality? As poor
Horace might say, *Adhuc sub judice lis est*.

XI Winning the Palm

Yes, I remember it well. The day the great thought struck. Spring, in its relentlessly depressing way, was bursting out all over, and reclining as I was on my chaise longue after my morning's work – a tedious First Holy Communion related visit to the little horrors in first class – a thought struck me. Even though I had enjoyed a light repast of lobster chowder and fricassee of chicken, washed down with a cheekily mellow Beaujolais, and felt suitably pleasured, and even though the distance to my desk seemed not just eight feet but several thousand miles, I felt compelled to put pen to paper.

God knows I could easily have deflected the conjuring tricks of whatever Muse sought to summon me to the task. Call it mere sloth or simply the shrinking effect of senescence, or just the Beaujolais. But what Juvenal calls *cacoethes scribendi* ('the itch for writing' – in deference to our younger confrères) generates its own momentum. And there it is: *quoad poeto perferam*.

The great truth that surfaced in my mind to create such unease was the need to help my confrères to focus on the central compulsion of so many of our lives: how to achieve life's great clerical ambition, the status of Parish Priest. This is a task, nay a vocation, to which so many have been so committed for so long, that its significance can sometimes pale into the background of our lives. What we are inclined to forget is that such an auspicious purpose demands something by way of support and confirmation. For that reason, I propose to offer a number of possible directives, or at least guidelines, to assist in that ineffable task. The trick is not how to become a PP – the sands of time achieve that – but how to wear it well. I have, of course, in the past volunteered my services in other appostie areas with, sad to say, little effect. For instance, I ventured to compile a list of apposite guidelines on clerical dress for the Episcopal Conference or any member thereof with the wit, if not the circumspection, to reconstitute something approaching diocesan statutes. The silence, I have to admit, was deafening: out of the Ordinary, one is tempted to say. But nothing daunted, *disce prodesse* is a tag that comes to mind, once more with feeling.

If for Cardinal Newman even a curacy had 'inexpressible charms', imagine the exhilaration of a parish of one's own, alleluia, alleluia. Yet intoxicating as the experience is, and I can hear hordes of thrusting curates salivating at the prospect, there is, let it be noted, a discretionary need to embrace a certain realism in this regard. Hence the following pastoral strategies for becoming a successful PP, based on long and – though I say so myself with my customary modesty – dignified if not edifying service in this august office.

At a Pope's coronation, a man walks in front scattering dust to remind the new incumbent that the glory of this world will come to nothing. It is a perceptive precedent. The temptation for the *parochus* is to arrive centre-stage with the roll of drums, the promise of great things, thunderous flashes from the wings, tumultous applause ringing in the ears ... and then, when the curtain is pulled back, you may find yourself standing there blinking in the light wondering what to do for an encore. Worse still, there may be no one in the hall.

There is a custom hallowed by time, certainly in rural parts, that the arrival of a PP should be definitively low-key if not discreet, a footnote rather than a banner headline. This does not of course compromise the historical nature of the event, but old hands like myself recognise from years of difficult experience that rural folk only rouse themselves to attend events associated with three basic hungers ... death, sex and guitar lessons.

A departing PP may, nudge-nudge, wink-wink, allow himself to be dragooned into what is presented to the uninitiated as a going-away function spontaneously organised by his grateful parishioners ('I couldn't let them down'). Par for the course and all that. But a corresponding function on arrival would only elicit to the power of a thousand the disparaging comment overheard in a churchporch after an overly-confident *parochus* had introduced himself to his nonchalant parishioners, 'Hasn't he great welcome for himself?' Rural folk have a sometimes disconcerting habit of keeping their admiration well under control.

Two bits of advice. First, never criticise the previous incumbent. If his reign was short, few will remember him after six months. If long, most will be anxious to forget about him. If of a distressingly appropriate duration, the reaction must be accordingly tempered to circumstance. If, as I have suggested before, he has left several monuments in cement in his memory, succeeding him will demand a certain perspicacity .

Usually help is at hand in the form of time and the elements. For one thing, *tempus* as we say *fugit*s. For another, great schemes massaged with a certain clerical torpor can become gloriously unstuck. Besides a few false compliments – 'a great man to make quick decisions' (mindless), 'he didn't suffer fools gladly' (never took advice), 'had a lot of different talents' (he fancied himself as a contractor, electrician, architect) – will generate sufficient opportunity, for those whose toes he metaphorically walked on, effectively to rubbish his achievements. Or you could devise some comparable technique to that of a new bishop during one of his first Masses, who, anxious to remember his predecessor who happened to be present, prayed 'for me your unworthy servant and for our former unworthy servant,' a deprecation at once devastatingly accurate and meritoriously symbolic.

Second piece of advice: Don't change anything for at least five years. It may be possible to tinker at the edges – paint a wall here, change the date of the parish pilgrimage to Knock there, even buy new baskets for the collection – but proclaiming an instant revolution invariably rebounds because it attributes mediocrity, not just to the previous incumbent, but to the parishioners. A course not to be prescribed for a rookie PP.

The trick is to embark on a blanket visitation as soon as possible.

An energetic cursory run around the parish will deflect from the tedium that comes from more measured visitation when they get to know you better or have more to say, and, if you get the tone of spontaneous sincerity just right, will elicit all the appropriately favourable comments: 'approachable', 'interested', 'energetic', 'sincere' and, invariably, 'a grand man' – on the proverbial basis that once smoke comes out of the chimney in the early morn you can sleep until noon. After such a blitz, it is usually possible not to darken doors for a period of at least four years. Say no more .

The two questions invariably asked about an incoming PP – is he fond of money? how long does it take him to say Mass? – require some evasive action. In the unlikely event of neither being a problem, *esto quod esse videris*. Irish people have a particular gift for sussing out in priests what Ovid called *amor sceleratus habendi*, 'the cursed passion for possessions'. The antidote is to refuse money at every opportunity. Work on the universally admirable tone of instinctive reluctance: 'out of the question, 'not my practice' or, better still, 'a matter of principle with me'. That kind of stuff. If, however, in the event you are unable to resist the purpley visage of the Liberator peering out from the new £20 banknote, don't pocket it too hastily. It's a dead giveaway. If you gain the reputation of being 'fond of money', they will begrudge you every penny. If you don't, you're made up for life.

Your first Mass is crucial, so pardon the directness of my approach. Don't tell them how happy you were in your last parish – they interpret it as a form of blackmail. Don't tell them how happy you are to be here – it convinces them that there's a question-mark over your last appointment. Simply introduce yourself or, rather, introduce yourself simply. A short resumé – place and date of birth, if you're on the right side of the 'Best before Seventy' mark, appointments, interests and so forth – will do the trick. The note to strike here is dullness. In the main people set a premium on dullness in their PPs. It's a kind of security blanket against the vapid trendiness that curates almost invariably strive to exude.

If, in due course, you happen to become a member of the diocesan chapter, or even a minor prelate, never suggest even obliquely that the honour is personal. In truth it never is, of course, in that honours in the Church are invariably conferred not for what you do but for what you haven't done. You always accept it, or rather you tell them you accept it, for the honour and glory of the parish – 'Lisnagoola always had a Canon' – or words to that effect. At the same time, you indicate that, even though you're next in line and have waited for several years for a confrère to retire or expire to create a vacancy, the accolade was completely unexpected, you're suitably overwhelmed and you'd be delighted if everyone continues to call you Fr Jack. In fact it's no harm at all to suggest that you felt so personally unworthy that the bishop had to twist your arm more than a bit to prevail on you to accept it. And even though the trip to Clery's in Dublin for a few fittings of the red soutane would set you back a few pounds, it would be worth it for the honour you brought to the parish and to the people. Indeed if a hint as broad as that can be given, can a suitable presentation be far behind? The trick is never to become like the American priest of whom it was said in his native Lisnagoola, 'All you have to call Mickeen Pat is 'Monsignor' and he relaxes completely.'

With my customary discretion, I hesitate to venture into tricky territory. But I must, I must. The modern emphasis on vices like empathy, sensitivity and 'owning the feminine side of your personality' is really a thinly-disguised conspiracy to allow the laity, particularly the weaker sex, to infiltrate positions of power and responsibility in the parish. The *General Instruction of the Roman Missal* consolingly states, for example, that it is 'at the discretion of the rector of the Church' that women may be appointed 'ministers outside the sanctuary'. The fact that this potentially radical instruction has been abrogated by subsequent law and custom need not be explicitly stated, and I have found it invaluable in tempering the excesses of the occasional liturgical Boadicea.

Two approaches are suggested on the basis that *si vis pacem, para bellum*: a firm hand and a penchant for the art of snag-hunting. The latter connotes the ability to listen sympathetically to any lay suggestion, however wayward or bizarre, while at the same time dredging the mind for some legal or liturgical snag. This enviable talent allows one to fall in love with a particular theory, for example, lay involvement in the Church, and even to talk about it endlessly while at the same time devising strategies to ensure that it will never be realised in substance: 'It wouldn't work here', 'We tried it before', 'There's a problem with insurance', and so on.

Finally, of course, there is the need to call it a day. There comes a stage when every year is a marker; every failure, an accusation; every funeral of a younger parishioner, a hidden irony; every family festivity, setting in relief the definite loneliness of an ageing celibate; every pastoral initiative emanating from the diocesan office, a confounded nuisance. And you find confrères of apposite vintage lapsing into a kind of transient gloom as they contemplate the dismal prospect of retirement, a fate apparently much worse than death.

Indeed, such is the mixture of gloom and resignation conjured up by that unholy spectre that elderly clerical gentlemen on the verge of superannuation can be seen traipsing indiscriminately around the place wearing puzzled expressions as if trying unsuccessfully to solve a problem in elementary algebra. The agenda of course is more personal: Where will I live? Who will look after me if I'm ill? Did I pull the front door after me? What is the meaning of life? Is it worth my while to change the car?

'There is nothing deader than a dead priest' a parishioner once said, demonstrating the bristly perspicacity of the countryman for the unvarying proprieties of rural life. But he was wrong. It's one thing to be 'gone but not forgotten'; it's even worse, it seems, to be 'forgotten but not gone'. Death can retrospectively encourage even the most critical to write straight with the crooked lines of a clerical life, often indeed without a hint of incongruity.

On the other hand, retirement, like marriage, invariably has a bad press. The limitations of one's successor, the pastoral equivalent of a variety of leaking roofs, and the disarming discomfort of playing not so much with a bad hand as with no cards at all, all arrive at one's door. Power, like victory, has many proud parents; retirement, like defeat, is invariably, an orphan. Indeed retirement for many is perceived as a veritable life sentence, as a kind of icon to which people defer but which everyone is half-expecting to be removed.

The alternative to the knacker's yard is to remain, as we rather inaccurately put it, 'in harness'. We can be persuaded to continue *quoad potero poteram* – usually for their own purposes, by our juniors of a very few years who are beginning to feel the draught and who need us as a kind of credibility buttress against the persistent goading of junior, nay minor, ecclesiastics of a thrusting disposition. And moreover we can be deluded by the remnants of our contracting fan-clubs to continue to put our wisdom and experience at the service of the Church. It is a refrain, indeed an anthem, that is literally music to our ears, but unfortunately experience indicates fairly conclusively that it is simply bad advice, like telling a schizophrenic that he really is Napoleon or God.

For one thing, time does take its toll. Energy is a progressively dissipating asset, and the reality is that in several of its constituent parts the tide is going out. Nature has rendered redundant the traditional prayer that accompanied the donning of the cincture: *Praecinge me, Domine, cingulo puritatis, et extingue in lumbis meis humoren libidinis.* I am reminded of a story told about a colleague who, over the course of a long life, struggled with that area of life we use words like concupiscence and libido to describe. I hesitate, as you might expect, to get into the dizzy details. At any rate, in his declining years, not having had what we used to call 'a bad thought' for over a period of six months, he invited his friends to celebrate the demise of concupiscence. Alas, it was not to be. The morning of the festivity each invitee received a telegram: 'Dinner indefinitely postponed. God between us and all harm.'

Clearly, drawing the line at seventy-five is (*pace* Pope John, Mr Deng of China and George Burns) drawing it in the wrong place. It is ten years the wrong side of its secular equivalent and five years in excess of what God defined as a long life. The truth is that the difference between sixty-five and seventy-five, like the difference between twelve and twenty-two, is not so much a decade as most of a lifetime. Somehow or other, on the wrong side of sixty-five, we tend to lose it a bit. It is not necessarily that the furniture upstairs gets shifted about, or that the escalator no longer goes to the top storey, or that we go, without putting a tooth in it, potty.

Yet, in truth, there is a predisposition to a form of mild dislocation that, for instance, can convince us that we are well nigh indispensable to the effective pastoring of the parish, the efficient administration of the diocese and the well-being of the universal Church. It is a condition not endemic to the Church. Eamon de Valera, by common consent, insisted on staying in power well past his sell-by date. Winston Churchill, past eighty, could not even recognise some members of his own cabinet and once, during a speech by the Minister for Agriculture, nudged the person next to him and whispered: 'Who is this chap?' There are episcopal analogies as well. A former bishop was once so gaga that every clerical personage of note who called to his home was able to issue a new batch of clerical changes and, on one noted occasion, there was a suspicion that the postman had actually moved several priests.

If I could digress for a moment. An associated condition is what I would call Post Retirement Vertigo (PRV) which, in later life, afflicts those who, though sufficiently integrated to accept retirement at the time, live to regret it. A lucidly thought out decision in retrospect is regarded as the equivalent of a rush of blood to the head, or being conned by the bishop, or bad theology, or whatever. An acquaintance of mine, a lapsed Chancellor, who is well into his eighties and enjoys the best of health and the financial appurtenances to go with it – an annual sight-seeing trip to the Canaries, a town-house, a satellite dish, a plentiful supply of Havana cigars – could, I imagine, be diagnosed as PRV positive. Even though he is the envy of all who know him, he pines for those fondly remembered bygone days when his looks, his beautiful singing voice and his collections were the envy of the diocese and, at that precise moment when fantasy gets the better of melancholia, he can advance the absurd proposition that he is willing and anxious to make a come-back, like a retired prize-fighter fondly imagining that he'd lick any of the present lot without even breaking into a sweat.

The truth is that retirement is not a kind of hell where useless priests are consigned because they had the ill luck to grow old before they died, nor a kind of purgatory though which they have to suffer the indignity of irrelevance, or even a kind of limbo where aged, unwanted and unloved clerics are aimlessly confined, but rather a kind of heaven-on-earth through which we escape from the frustrations and the acerbities of our present existence.

For instance, take curates. Most of us, in our declining years, have had to endure the undignified spectacle of what can best be described as a creeping coup. In effect, the Church has been taken over by curates.

Time was when PPs had the power: curates were told what to do and invariably did it. Time was when the title 'Canon' was an honour to be embraced, not an object of fun to be ridiculed, and those on whom this canonical garter was conferred were greeted with pertinent awe rather than the present contemporary snigger. Time was when curates were the canonical equivalent of the shop-boy, always there when they were needed but never allowed to order anything. Now not only do they insist on taking over the shop but they feel compelled to turn it into the liturgical equivalent of McDonald's.

Could I perhaps digress once more? By way of counteracting what is now perceived as declining morale among priests, and by way of getting the barque of Peter back on an even keel after the excitement of recent times, could I make a suggestion. Hollywood has its Oscars, New York its Grammys and London its Baftas. The Queeen has her Honours list, the Pope his *Bene Merentis*, so why not perhaps *Intercom* its Priests of the Year Awards? (P.O.T.Y. would make a neat acronym.)

The National Conference of Priests could organise the actual ceremony – wouldn't it give them something to do? – and friends, relatives, confrères and significant others could be invited to ensure that someone would actually turn up. Laypeople –

whom we're trying to involve in everything under the sun with a sense of urgency – could nominate priests for the different categories and this would ensure that the Plymouth Argyles as well as the Manchester Uniteds would be represented, the Achonrys as well as the Tuams, that outside lefts as well as inside rights – if you get my drift – could have the ball at their feet, that the footsoldiers as well as the domestic prelates would have a place in the sun.

If memory serves me right, there's an Episcopal Commission for the Clergy somewhere and, if there is, couldn't the Chairman, if there is a Chairman, present the awards? Clerical stars in the Irish firmament could open the envelopes and announce the winners. The supreme accolade or rosette would be for The Most Wonderful Priest of the Year. For obvious reasons this would be confined to those ordained before 1962 and candidates would possess the qualities that are most admired in Irish priests: benignity, cuteness, dullness and a very black suit. Lesser accolades would be for:

(i) the Prudent Priest of the Year – requisite qualities to include: an ability to ingratiate himself with the local Ordinary, a refusal to attempt anything that might even be vaguely interpreted as novel, caution, and the ownership of a Toyota Corolla.

(ii) the With-it Priest of the Year – a 2-litre Passat with polyphonic stereo and car telephone, an Apple Mac with QuarkXPress 3.1, an impressive c.v. of foreign holidays, a wardrobe with several colour co-ordinated ensembles, a shower every morning and shares in Old Spice.

(iii) the Without-It Priest of the Year – a boisterous self-confidence, a cosmic incompetence, an inability to hold two thoughts concurrently, and a complete lack of imagination.

(iv) the Still-With-Us Priest of the Year – for the most notorious well-past-retirement-date priest who, despite great odds, has managed to hold on to both the parish and the parochial house.

(v) The Most Difficult Curate Award – a long nomination list here, and in later life the same fun people will be eligible for The Most Difficult PP of the Year Award.

(vi) Canon of the Year – the tastiest accolade of all, the inside track with the Ordinary, the admiration of both the ordinary and the Ordinary and a singular sense of the extraordinary.

(vii) and finally, the prestigious Hall of Fame Award – a healthy disregard for the laity, an antipathy to curates, a biretta, a *Liber Usualis*, and a bottomless pit of tedious stories about Maynooth, a diocese where he worked in England and his inaccurate version of his own imaginary achievements. This category would be confined to legends in their own minds. The P.O.T.Y. Awards would, of course, be sponsored by Church and General with the two birds sitting on an apt symbol. Suggestions on a postcard, please to The Editor, *Intercom*.

But where was I? Oh, yes, curates. In the last twenty years or so, under the guise of such questionable slogans as 'the people of God' and 'involving the laity', curates have actually taken over control of the Church. Under the guise of co-responsibility, or if the truth were told, bishops pandering to curates' demands, parishes have been in effect divided into independent republics. Marriages can now be validly contracted without the PP dispensing faculties; parish cheque books are now in curates' hands, and, horror of horrors, curates now earn practically as much as their canonical superiors.

This appalling vista was visited on the unsuspecting PPs in our diocese through a series of meetings where sermonettes were preached on the financial implications of the clergy as 'brothers in Christ', and the asking of theorical questions like 'What would Jesus say?', as if that had anything to do with it.

How times have changed. After half-a-lifetime being treated like a recalcitrant altar-boy who had just spilled a cruet of wine on the new carpet, I am condemned until retirement to be berated by ordained spaniels who have transmogrified themselves into terriers! Forgive me, dear reader, I sometimes get quite carried away.

So you can see that the following alternatives are on offer: either an uneasy truce with a thrusting curate who has difficulty getting Lauds and Vespers said but no problem lecturing men who have spent a lifetime on their knees, who is more often on the golf course than in the parish, visits the pub more often than the church, a teller of risqué jokes at weddings ... or a pleasant retirement. Which should I choose?

Life with a curate? I don't think so. At best an uneasy alliance under a heavy weight of varying perceptions and perspectives or, at worse, the diocesan rotweiller. Retirement? At best an opportunity to pursue a lifelong hobby, develop new interests, visit the Holy Land. Or at worse, having absolutely nothing to do.

Dum vivimus, vivamus ... while we have life, let us live. *Post tot naufragia portum.*

XII   A Passion for the Purple

An insidious rumour, fuelled by the uncertainty that surrounds the coming of an *episcopus* from the East, has put it about that there are plans to scupper the Diocesan Chapter. Whether such a precipitate action would fall within the authority of a local Ordinary is a moot point for the canonists, if such there are anymore, to ponder. Whether it is necessary to disband a grouping whose function has, albeit juridically, disappeared, is a question for realists, if such there are anymore, to consider.

A new Code, a more perceptive laity, a modern distrust of formality, a contemporary derision for the conferring of empty honours, and a manifest decline in the popularity of fancy dress, are said to have contributed to a perceptible lessening in prestige for the once hallowed office of 'Canon'. The situation has reached a depressing nadir when a confrère, recently appointed to this exalted and traditionally prestigious position, cautioned his honoured parishioners to continue calling him 'Father Mick', not as a political ploy to ingratitate himself with his people – as I counselled earlier – but because he actually meant it!

It is a sad business. On dark, drizzly days when the spirit droops, the telly is on the blink, and the prospect of another interminable meeting with progressively recalcitrant lay people further blights an already bleak week, God and the prospect of a Canon's soutane – with red buttons down the front and silky red satin peering demurely from under the flaps – keep me going.

Having a priest in the family, like an inside toilet and a bull in the yard, was in rural parts always regarded as a signal honour. Having a parish priest was riches indeed, often in more ways

than one. But having a Canon was the ultimate in ecclesiastical
and social grandeur. And now with the almost universal availability of colour photography – First Holy Communion, Confirm-
ations, Weddings, the list is gratifyingly endless – the prospect
of such an honour constitutes in anticipation a certain restrained
compensation for the essential tediousness of my declining
years.

A spate of recent retirements and the timely, though of course
regrettable, demise of a few senior confrères still in harness,
have narrowed the field considerably. I am now, I would esti-
mate, no more than 18 places from a Canon's biretta, 33 from the
Archdeacon's chair, and 34 from the grandeur of being Dean of
the Diocese.

You may, kind reader, wonder why with my customary modesty I have no ambitions for higher honours, the swish of a mon-
signorial cassock in unrelievedly resplendent red, or the delicious prospect of a purple cummerbund to offset the effect of my
considerable paunch. The reasons are two. One, it is an unspoken
ordinance in clerical company, not even in jest, to own such ambitious thoughts. And even if one actively pursued such heights,
as some of the confrères so obviously, indeed enthusiastically,
do – long time, no See – any suggestion of an impending call to
the Navan Road would be waved aside as being beyond one's
humility even to contemplate. There is, as we all know, a studied
reluctance to embrace office that has become a prerequisite for
promotion. Two, holding my hand firmly on my heart, I do not
believe that I am sufficiently unremarkable to expect such high
office.

I do not jest. Predictions by media or local commentators as to
who will fill what position are nearly always exactly wrong. The
reason is that it is not always noted by casual and not-so-casual
observers that ability is the greatest impediment to high office in
the Church. Despite occasional aberrations, those most likely, as
most incumbencies demonstrate, to be appointed to positions of
responsiblity are those least suitable. Putting the squarest of
square pegs in the roundest of round holes is a matter not of
misjudgement but of principle. Bulls, if you'll pardon the ex-

pression, with an embarrassing history of collisions behind them, will invariably be appointed to run china-shops. Cuckoos will be expected to build complex and sophisticated nests. Filigree Siberian hamsters will be asked to guard chicken coops.

I labour the point. This policy, again to the casual observer, may smack of inefficiency or mismanagement or even irresponsibility. But that surface reaction would be a misreading of what is an established, long-term plan. If the holiest, most personable, most able, most communicative hard worker was invariably appointed bishop, if the most suitable priest was always appointed *parochus*, if the most talented curates were encouraged to develop their individual gifts, then the Church as we know and love it would begin to fall apart at the seams.

One, because disaffection among the clergy, the avoidance of which is a *sine qua non* for the survival of the institution, would be rampant. We would complain... openly. Two, because the principle of seniority, on which rests the entire superstructure of civilisation, would be irreparably breached. I might never become a Canon. And three, because a well-organised, efficiently managed Church might give the impression that it was merely a human institution. Its survival might not be invariably explained by the presence of the Holy Spirit.

But I wander, I wander. Where was I? Oh yes! So my ambition, if such an ugly word has to be worn, is some day to become not an honorary member of the Pontiff's household or the Ordinary of even an insignificant See, but a member of our august Chapter. It is my dream – and this of course is completely confidential – to wear one day, with a certain restrained panache, the red-buttoned soutane with a scarlet flap cursorily thrown back over the shoulder for prelatorial effect, and to hold the red biretta between thumb and index finger as is the sacrosanct rubrical requirement from time immemorial. I take Thomas O'Donnell's point that we should be content with little and prepared to 'labour in honourable dependence upon episcopal authority', and that seeking to obtain a rich benefice or to be decorated with honours is unbecoming for men of the cloth. And so it is. But is it a great sin, I find myself asking as the years tumble away in front of me, to yearn for that day to come when I will be licenced to wear the rochet? While the mere surplice, according to James O'Kane's definitive *Rubrics of the Roman Missal*, signifies the innocence and purity with which we are clothed in putting on the second Adam, the rochet, a vestment that belongs properly to bishops, can be worn by inferior dignitaries with special permission from the Holy See. I have investigated this happy dispensation in some detail and I am informed on high authority that, in special cases, such authority can be delegated to the local Ordinary by the Holy See.

In my present traditional raiment of unrelieved black I am, I must admit, a poor advertisement for the contemporary clerical excesses of sartorial elegance. Indeed to describe my personal appearance as unimpressive would not seem to be unduly censorious. And yet, call it an old man's fancy if you will, it does not seem an unwarranted aspiration to want to wear a mere speckle of red before the dark, dank clay of Lisnagoola rests on my weary bones.

So it is my intention, while I await the demise or retirement of a mere 18 of my revered *parochi*, or rather *parochorum*, to prepare for that great and good day by concentrating on three strategies hallowed by time and custom.

One, is to pray for the health to achieve that first requirement, *casus foederis*, for membership of the Chapter, old age. A more careful diet with a closer eye on my consumption of polyunsaturates, and some amenable exercise taken in small portions, would seem to fit the bill.

Two, is to say or do nothing exceptional. After almost a lifetime of embracing the definitive clerical philosophy of *festina lente*, I don't intend to blow it on the run-in. I intend to spend my remaining years ensconced in my fireside chair, expending just enough energy to keep my pipe alight, inviting the local Ordinary to the occasional culinary diversion, agreeing volubly with everything our Holy Father says, while finding it inopportune at this point in time to do what he wants, keeping tabs on the more disruptive members of my congregation by repeating

in a thousand forms that most effective of pastoral put-downs
'We tried that before and it didn't work', and generally keeping
firmly in place every last shutter of life.

Three, is to hope and pray that in the intervening years the worst
won't happen and the Chapter be abolished before I get there. In
my earlier more spirited years, my recurring nightmare was to
live to see compulsory celibacy abrogated but to be too decrepit
to celebrate adequately its passing. A more recent nightmare is
to hear the Pope announce the abolition of Chapters in the intervening days between the bishop confirming the good news of
my appointment and the actual announcement. Stranger things
have happened. The unfortunate breaching of the Berlin Wall
has sent waves of giddiness through erstwhile impregnable in-
stitutions. And with the symbolic coming of the third millenni-
um, the Pontiff may be pressured, for whatever dubious reason,
to abolish Chapters as a grand but fatal gesture to mark a new
frontier of collegiality or vulnerability or some such twaddle.

I know, as I mentioned earlier, that at a Pope's coronation, a man
walks in front scattering dust, reminding the new prince that the
glory of this world will come to nothing. But as the late Andy
Warhol, that guru of the plastic arts, once put it, 'Everyone
should be famous for five minutes.' In my lighter moments I
sometimes feel that everyone should be an Archdeacon, even for
a little while. I know that such an approach might usher in a
dubious spectacle of a kind of canonical musical chairs. But if it
would not appear unduly disedifying, it could afford those of us
on our last legs even a short time in the sun.

I offered this and other related suggestions for consideration at a
Council of Priests's meeting, but my initiative was not *in universo*
favourably received. A confrère, diffident almost to the point of
extinction, roused himself to object to the general tenor of my
rumblings. More specifically, he took umbrage at my suggestion
that the office of Archdeacon should, like the Presidency of the
European Community, revolve periodically among the *parochi*.

His last public utterance, reputedly sometime in the Sixties, was
in response to the rather anarchic suggestion common in that in-

solent decade that PPs should retire at seventy. My friend, for such I then presumed him to be, objected to the prospect of the knacker's yard at the absurdly premature age of three score and ten, biblical precedents notwithstanding. The very thought of a PP being metaphorically stamped with a 'Best Before Seventy' brand was a consummation devoutly to be avoided. At forty, no more than a callow youth, his curious intervention had at least then the merits of disinterestedness, in that what we fondly but inaccurately imagine 'the best years of priesthood' were still ahead of him.

Not so the august position of Archdeacon to which honour he is at present edging up the avenue. Was anything sacred anymore? Did I realise the implications of my outrageous thesis – for the diocese, the Church, the world and even possibly for the future of civilisation itself? Was it not of such a dreadful prospect that Yeats surely must have written his prophetic words 'Things fall apart; the centre cannot hold'? Hyperbole rules, okay?

In my defence, I tried to point out that I was trying to offset the influence of thrusting young bloods among the brethren who despise any kind of honour – especially those out of reach – and have been known to poke fun at some of the necessary appurtenances of canonical status – the dash of red, the purple cummerbund, titles like 'Venerable' and so on. I was in effect merely trying to suggest more amenable forms for traditional truths. However, a somewhat withering look indicated that I had once again disappointed yet another erstwhile friend. But I suffer on. My reward, as another colleague somewhat dubiously suggested, would be in the next life.

Such preoccupations could be lightly dismissed as no more than another delightful reminder of the curious eccentricities to which the brethren seem definitively prone. In a world where the future seems progressively more improbable, and in a Church rapidly contracting out of sight, in influence if not in numbers,. it may in the circumstances all seem peculiarly Neroic, a particularly comic form of clerical fiddling while the flames are rising around us. At the same time, I hold my ground. Canon O'Donnell might not think too much of this form of ambition raising its ugly head, but for those who, like Horace, can point to *integer vitae scelerisque purus*, it could be the nearest we might get to *monumentum aere perennius*.

There is too the not inconsiderable point that this passion for the purple is shared by the laity. An example illustrates the point. In our local paper, which achieves such effortless inanity that it would glory in the appellation 'rag', there is a widely-read section unimaginatively entitled 'Lisnagoola Notes and News'. Of course nothing of great import condescends to occur in this innocuous bailiwick. Indeed the first edition of what was intended to be an annual yearbook by an enthusiastic predecessor, gobbled up so much news that a decade later I have still not rushed a second edition into print. Yet week after week, a series of 'Notes' if not 'News', a blend of incontrovertible fact and non-litigious fiction, appears (and that is the accurate word for it) in the local *Herald*.

With a flawless feel for fun and frivolity, pride of place is usually given to a local death which, regardless of circumstance, is invariably contrived 'to cast a gloom over the entire community' and 'a large and representative gathering' invariably attends the subsequent obsequies. If the local equivalent of Jack the Ripper had passed on to his reward, the tribute would be no less fulsome. Visitors from London or New York usually enjoy 'a welcome break' ; the exploits of the local draughts team, in what are inaccurately called 'Community Games' , a sporting oxymoron, which are in effect a pernicious forum for interparish rivalry and intrigue, are depressingly chronicled in quite tortuous detail; and to fill the allotted space a few creative events are related: the manager of the parish team upbraids his ineffective charges to make this the year Lisnagoola Juniors carve their name with pride on the divisional trophy, the winning of a 50p first prize for a pound pot of gooseberry jam at a local agricultural show, and the birth of twin calves to some hitherto innocuous Lisnagoola heifer.

But I wander. In a recent edition, an item which appeared in the Kilsakeery Notes created something of a stir. In the June diocesan changes, a confrère was, *O felix culpa*, appointed a member of the

Diocesan Chapter. This felicitous event, which incidentally
moved me one step towards realising the second part of life's
ambition, came, if the truth were told as distinct from being alluded to, by way of the imposition on the said pastor of a retired
Canon as a half-curate. The unexpected ecclesiastical congruence of two canons in one parish was made something of a meal
of in *The Herald*.

This 'note', tucked away between comparably irrelevant events,
a death and a marriage as it happened, generated the expected
local interest. Even though my two confrères are in effect only a
full Canon between them, since both are merely half-Canons,
the elder honorary, the younger imaginary, this detail has thankfully been lost on even the most learned of clerical groupies. It
was the talk of the place. 'A singular honour for the parish' people called it, even though there were two of them. Tradition had
it, of course, that Kilsakeery always 'got a canon' but two, as the
Americans rather inaccurately and inelegantly say, was something else altogether. Neighbouring Addergoole, it was said by
those in the know and confirmed by the local historian in a letter
to *The Herald*, had both a Canon and a Doctor of Canon Law in
the thirties but, like Palm Sunday and St Patrick's Day falling on
the same day in 1938, that was regarded as something of an
aberration. The common consensus was that Kilsakeery's was
the greatest honour.

There ensued, as fate or rather providence would have it, quite a
debate on the role, indeed the significance of the Diocesan
Chapter. Naturally, with the laity's limited knowledge of the
impressive liturgical, administrative and canonical functions associated with this high office, and the propensity of modern
adult education classes for avoiding, for some inexplicable reason,
the more important issues of Church life, the debate was thin on
substance. However, their hearts were, as we say, in the right
place. The laity, unlike some of my junior confrères, who seem
to regard the whole issue as an excuse for indulging their effortlessly juvenile humour, has an instinctive feel for the significance of high office in the Church and the appurtanances that
are associated with it. It was said 'it did something' for people to
see a priest wearing purple. What that was never became clear

but you could sense that it was important from the restrained, even solemn tone in which it was said.

Memories were awakened of clerical dignitaries from the past who travelled to Dublin to order the red soutane and the frilly item of lingerie that went with it, and people remembered (like when President Kennedy was killed) the fateful day when Canon Killeen 'appeared' in the red soutane with the red buttons down the front of it and the distinctive way he nonchalantly threw back the silky red lapels over his shoulders.

Naturally, noting the congenital ignorance of the laity in such matters, there was some confusion over the colours of the vestments. It was debated in the local hostelry as to whether the vestment colour the priest wore at Mass indicated canonical status. Did the vestment colour indicate that the wearer was curate, PP, archdeacon, dean, chancellor, bishop or pope? Mickey Griffin, who incidentlly is not among our most loyal patrons in every sense of the word, advanced the thesis one night in the local hostelry that canons wore purple, bishops wore red, curates wore green and the pope wore white. His assembled entourage nodded sanguinely into their pint glasses. Someone remembered, however, that our Fr Derek had a penchant for startling white vestments, a fad caught incidentally in a past existence from some wealthy dowager in Buffalo whose patronage he unstintingly curried, and even though he has something of a reputation for acting in the role of the Holy Father, this had the effect of putting a question-mark over the whole thesis. Mickey was delegated to ask his wife Detta, the president of the local Legion Presidium, to seek my counsel. I regarded the invitation not just as an opportunity to clarify some important issues, but a veritable *sensus fidelium* enjoining us to tamper at our peril with titles hallowed by centuries of tradition.

Another result of this topical debate was the very apposite question as to what exactly a Canon does, as distinct from being admired for his own sake. 'What is a canon for?' a perspicacious parishioner asked. This afforded me the opportunity to impart the relevant instruction by way of an extended Sunday homily. I specified the four main areas of happy duty for those raised to the dignity of membership of the Chapter.

One, the significance of presiding in the cathedral at specified liturgical functions, though somewhat curtailed in recent years. Two, the authority to elect a temporary administrator of the diocese in the event of the demise of the Ordinary, in dioceses where the council of priests had not as yet usurped that function. Three, the accumulated administrative, pedagogical and spiritual wisdom which the bishop taps into, albeit at progessively and distressingly less frequent intervals. And four, the general ambience of dignity and the aura of refinement that Canons exude.

Folk tradition, too, turned up the custom of wearing the ermine which, for confrères of a lesser vintage, was a shoulder cape of white weasel fur worn and, if I may say so without being gratuituously disedifying, cutting quite a sartorial dash at liturgical functions. My curate, Fr Derek, evinced a certain interest in this liturgical garment and then, as is his wont, passed a perfidious remark about wolves in sheep's clothing and once more laughed uproariously at his own joke. If he had intimated anything even vaguely like the appropriate response a mere curate should have to such matters, I would have produced for his edification from my private closet the very vestment he found so irritatingly humorous, purchased through a proxy at an auction some four decades earlier as a long-term investment for my life's second greatest ambition. It is perhaps something of an irony of history that the said ermine is still in immaculate condition but a general council of the Church intervened to deny me the honour of wearing it. *O tempora, O mores.*

XIII 'Mature in years and spotless of reputation'

'Man to the hills, woman to the shore', or so the proverb goes. But the turn of the year draws me inexorably to Lisnagoola strand to savour the tactile freshness of the season, to tread, in Heaney's phrase, 'the fallow avenue' between parched dunes and salivating wave, to walk this place in thanksgiving. There is a sensual excitement here, a feeling that God's design reaches a still pivot before nature commands the confidence to turn winter into spring. The placid sands of Dunmoran, gently disturbed into rippled patterns by the receding tide, predicate a grandeur if not of God at least of the kind of land and seascape that in another day and place got the better of Hardy and Brontë and made them pay their fulsome dues to acquisitive nature. But pardon such eclectic allusions, after all this is not Dorset or the Yorkshire Moors, but homely Lisnagoola looking its best on a spring day.

There is, Ecclesiastes reminds us, a time for everything under heaven. This, I reflect, is a time for gardening and for golfing; that time of the year when we retrieve from the attic the varied artefacts that help hard-pressed rural pastors to come to terms with one of the great mysteries of parish life: how will I pass the summer?

There was a time, when all we had to do was to mention vaguely to the housekeeper that there was 'a bit of a stretch in the evenings' and the life-support system of the rural pastor was instantly retrieved from attic or basement. Golf-clubs were lovingly polished, fishing-rods assembled and swished into top form, gardening implements laid out like sentries, the pony's harness Brilloed into life. O happy days! It was a time when we enjoyed, if that's not putting too fine a point on it, the varied ministrations of that devoted sorority.

Of course, it was never easy, as Canon O'Donnell points out, to select a housekeeper who would 'neither spoil one's stomach nor violate the statutes': someone who in the words of the Third Council of Baltimore ought to be mature in years and spotless of reputation, *integerima fama et maturioris aetatis*. According to the Council of Trent, there could be no woman in a priest's house who would be likely to give rise to suspicion against him. This, as countless local statutes specified, meant someone 'passing forty' though the Maynooth Statutes, while they specified that a priest shall not retain any woman as a comrade or companion in his own house under pain of suspension *ferendae sententiae*, simply indicated that housekeepers should be 'in so far as possible, of a rather advanced age', *in quantum possibile, provectioris aetatis*. Other qualities included being 'attentive to her religious duties, not affected or negligent in her dress, modest, civil to visitors and neither a chatterbox nor a newsmonger'. She had, of course, her own quarters with, as the Statutes required, a separate staircase. Indeed, when I showed Fr Derek around the Parochial House on his first visit, I was appalled to discover that his ignorance of the Statutes was such that he thought my explanation for the second staircase was given in jest. Just as later, when I explained why a temporary maid, of unhappy memory and alas! the wrong side of forty, was in the back seat of my car as we returned from shopping. The phrase *solus cum sola* was a complete mystery to him and the appropriate Statute governing such travel in the presence of a member of the opposite sex, Number 15 incidentally, meant absolutely nothing to him. Nor indeed did the precautions towards *ancillae vel oeconomae* that experts like O'Donnell suggest we should observe in this regard:

> to be rather distant and reserved with her, not to hear her confession, not to make her a confidante of one's troubles, not to discuss parochial affairs with her or in her presence, not to seek information from her, never to allow her to interfere directly or indirectly with visitors or parishioners, to give her neither presents nor much praise, not to scold her or to bring tears to her eyes, to trust her and leave all the details

of housekeeping to her, but at the same time to use pass-books and account books, and to keep letters and money under lock and key.

There was a time too when many of my generation thought the ministrations of housekeepers was an area of life replete with possibilities. If the maid in question had a clear hand, she could attend to such distractions as writing out baptismal certificates, copying lists of Masses to be forwarded to the Friars and licking the appropriate stamps and envelopes. Indeed, if her hand was sufficient, she could transcribe one's sermons without the effort of moving from a fireside chair. Or for that matter, if she was sufficiently robust, she could undertake the onerous task of carrying the clerical bag of golfclubs up hill and down dale, and varied other exertions that often task the clerical constitution.

It is, alas, no longer the case. In those innocent days we could not possibly have foreseen the construction that our illiberal age would put on the happy enjoyment of basic human comforts and the consolation of having someone to answer the Rosary or pare one's corns. Now, despite keeping the relevant Statutes and taking the most obvious precautions, the priest's housekeeper has become an endangered species on the Irish clerical land-scape. Once a much sought after position in rural Irish life, its status has diminished considerably in recent years. To such an extent that any candidate for the position with even a vague notion of what it is to make tea or boil an egg is hunted for her signature like soccer prima donnas in the Premier League.

Once they ministered respectfully and graciously to almost every clerical need; opening the door to visitors and unerringly determining whether the arrivals were guests to be welcomed or malcontents to be banished; knocking gently at the door of 'the study' so as not to unduly disturb the *Parochus* ensconced in his easy chair; and bearing trays of willow-patterned crockery, rhubarb-tart and homemade buns. God be with the days when the porridge was lovingly made every morning, the milk gently tepid for the All-Bran, and the fire cheerfully blazing by the time the morning ablutions were complete. What a joy it was to stroll through a tilled and tended garden reading matins, to gaze with the psalmist 'on the earth and all its fullness', to survey a weed-less tapestry of vegetable, flower and fruit, giving honour and glory to God, not to speak of a veritably endless supply of fresh vegetables. Now the garden lies fallow and over-grown, a fitting monument to the new breed. They tend to be younger, lazier and less biddable than their more matronly antecedents.

A Youth Employment Grant (to the tune of a £30 a week salary supplement) encouraged me to employ Debbie. The experiment was not a success. Invariably exhausted from some post-midnight tryst that culminated in a loud and late return on a Honda 1500, she condescended to pull herself out of bed sometime before noon. The air was continually punctuated by a highpitched scream from the kitchen to the effect that 'there's someone at the door' as if the loud knocking could be misconstrued for a posse of leprechauns making fishsoup or whatever. A request to answer the door usually received the rejoinder that if the dinner was to be on time 'she couldn't make bits of herself'. Resisting the temptation to do just that, I pointed out calmly that if she got up in time ... I return to the sittingroom thanking God or rather the Church for the great gift of celibacy and wondering vaguely how I could get rid of this youthful Amazon whom the Minister for Labour had somehow insinuated into my once tranquil life.

A confrère, not noted for his tolerance, once parted company from his housekeeper by throwing a bucket of water over her in the bed because she wouldn't get up for Mass and his breakfast. In the event such drastic measures were unnecessary as Debbie, after sulking about the fact that she wasn't used to bringing in turf, decided to make her fortune in England. She received my blessing, parishioners found it much easier to get through on the phone, my life returned to a comforting monotony, and I became converted to the belief that in relationships there is such a thing as 'irretrievable breakdown'.

After 'divorce' remarriage would seem to tempt fate, so I opted for a 'go-it-alone' policy. Again, not a complete success. Exasperation with Debbie was replaced with exasperation with my own curious inability to maintain even moderately hygienic conditions in the more public parts of the house. Each morning's social liturgy consisted of spreading yesterday's copy of the *Irish Independent* in front of the fire and building a pyramid of ashes in its centre, carefully lifting it by its extremities and rushing headlong down the garden to deposit it out of sight. A teabag was placed in an outsize mug, bearing a vaguely risqué slogan, which was filled with boiling water, and two toasted slices of white bread, buttered and marmaladed, were consumed over a two-bar electric fire. The soutane, that erstwhile 'garment of commitment' from seminary days, became a popular morning attire under the essential Crombie until the turf kindled and the bones thawed.

After a lonely Eucharist and a perusal of post and paper, it was almost time to prepare what I laughlingly described as 'lunch'. This consisted of frozen peas, potatoes and steak, a carton of yogurt and another teabag in another mug. My desk, piled high with tumuli, became a paper forest through which I trekked endlessly and fruitlessly. My bedroom, in which an articulated truck could turn without any great difficulty, took on the semblance of a launderette devastated in an explosion. Toilet-rolls began to appear on the mantelpiece in the sittingroom, dust could be seen on dust, green fungi began to appear on unwashed utensils, and lines of gelled cartons of milk stood beside the fridge like those furry sentries outside Buckingham Palace. It was time, I considered, to seek some assistance.

Out of the bleak mid-Winter, Mary arrived in the form of a daily help. This seemed the ideal solution. If marriage, as Shaw remarked, would always be popular because it combined the maximum of temptation with the maximum of opportunity, the daily help seems the answer to every priest's prayer in that it combines the minimum of inconvenience with the minimum of discomfort. Passing encounter is always easier on the constitution than total commitment. Mary's arrival meant that dinner was edible, that I received accurate, up-to-the-minute reports on the happenings of the parish, and that I retained the full freedom of the house, in that I didn't need to squint around corners before sprinting the short distance between crucial antechambers. Out of such profound considerations, a modicum of clerical contentment is accomplished.

Another possibility suggests itself. A confrère, a serendipity-freak, has discovered to his delight that many years ago a religious congregation of sisters was founded in Spain to minister domestically to priests, a truly admirable apostolate that has not for some reason yet reached this island of saints and scholars. I have no doubt that, as religious orders were invariably founded in answer to some pressing need in the Church, it might just be possible for some bishop to found a new order of mature women, who would in line with the usual statutes, minister domestically to the priests of Ireland. An indigenous spirituality could be developed, an appropriate support system by way of indulgences and so forth could be put in place, and draft statutes drummed up by some redundant canon lawyer. Perhaps the first foundation could be made up of nuns unhappy with the feminist ethos sweeping through convent life at the moment.

God be with the days when a religious sister would lovingly shine the life out of every clerical spoon, starch the serviette until it could stand on its own, and face every moving utensil in the direction of 'His Reverence'. Now, in visiting a convent, you have practically to prepare your own meals, and asking for a cup of tea and a heated scone is dismissed as part of a patriarchal legacy from the dim and distant past. Which reminds me about a colleague's experience in a convent in the west of Ireland. The said cleric, who had a weakness for a portion of prunes before breakfast, enjoyed this exotic fare for many years, remarking continuously on their consistent quality. Eventually he discovered that, every morning long before the cock crew, some ministering angel would delicately insert a plastic straw into the said prunes to ease away their wrinkles so that they could appear less intimidating on the breakfast table. The story, apocryphal or not, has a warming air about it. Now that's the kind of healthy attitude that should imbue the proposed foundation. *Integerrima fama et maturioris aetatis* and more besides.

XIV Strange hybrids

Unlike Heinz, priests come in more than 57 different varieties. Though we present in our black suits and metallic Toyota Corollas as definitively assembly-line products, albeit in various stages of youth or decrepitude, the actual truth is as always much stranger than the perceived fiction. Behind the all-weather exterior, which we often contrive to present to an unsuspecting public, lies a superfluity of character, in the wider sense of that word. The black or progressively grey suit can disguise a motley patchwork of indivuals.

Despite the often bizarre 'formation', if the word doesn't stretch the reality, to which many of us inadvertantly or reluctantly submitted, and the essential dullness of mind and spirit readily accredited to the ineffable tedium of the clerical life, nature – like the memory in the potter's clay – has in desperate circumstances a cheering habit of gloriously reasserting itself. We are, after all, in our various shapes, sizes and contours, fragments of that humanity to which Irenaeus so uncharacteristically witnessed.

But within the mad and luminous variety of humankind to whom God in his innocence directed a particular call, significant categories are known to emerge – a subspecies, if you like, of a certain genus. A particular species, though chosen first only by way of explication, is the priest-teacher. Not to be confused, of course, with the part-time teacher-of-religion-cum-curate who is to the real thing what inanimate clay was to Heidegger.

The priest-teacher inhabits that effete, though now generally re-dundant, world of yesteryear for which a pair of shoes left out-side their doors to be polished is a ready metaphor. Persilled

napkins lovingly starched and ironed, a civilised seniority seat-
ing system at meals, separate dainty little pots of tea, a motor
superfluous to personal or vocational need, the obligatory inadequate accommodation in which they are forced to survive, un-
amenable toiletry conditions, and the stale and doubtful joy of
male community life. The kind of world where, as Clive James
would say, the laundry box exists to reassure its inhabitants that
there is a linen room somewhere which they will die without
ever having to visit. In more innocent days they were grandly
dubbed 'Professors', before the questionable boon of free education and the consequent advent of veritable hosts of lay-teach-
ers, male and female, invaded their private and fragile world.

Despite the lessening of status and the partial application for
membership of the human race it has necessitated, it is still possible to spot priest-teachers at some distanee. The full-flowing
soutane with the lapels self-consciously thrown back over the
shoulders – once the definitive uniform and doubling as central
heating and a semi-liturgical chalk-apron – has given way to the
black American suit picked up at an outrageously giveaway
price in some 'army surplus' Californian store. This grotesquely
shiny vestment is not to be confused with its duller Irish coun-
terpart that shines with age, usually from the posterior out-
wards, and in a later existence is known to turn at least forty
shades of green. Examples are modelled at most conferences. It
is the clerical equivalent of what in the rag trade is called 'pre-
faded demin'.

That shiny American suit is, of course, one of the unfortunate
products of the annual junket to the US: usually balmy
California or, when they don't know any better, sweaty New
York. Come June and the Aer Lingus Jumbos are full of priest-
teachers ready to freeload for the summer in some benign and
lucrative parish. It is the best of all possible clerical worlds.
While the monthly cheques from the Department of Education
pile up neatly on the mantelpiece at home, and erstwhile ac-
quaintances are remade with ageing American dowagers of
great Catholicity and unlimited lucre, the *raison d'être* for this
annual pilgrimage to the California sun is of course to sample
the pastoral scene to which they would be more permanently

committed if God had not called them to greater things, teaching irregular French verbs or explaining the *copal* 'is' to bored adolescents. There is too the not inconsiderable advantage of experiencing at first hand such pastoral novelites as baptising children and burying the dead and thereby preparing, in the long term of course, for whatever prestigious parish to which tradition and nature deemed them to be entitled, a prospect for which they continually *sotto voce* indicate their readiness if not enthusiasm while at the same time displaying a marked reluctance actually to move.

Then, after a few months of golf, travel, an appropriate tinge of brown from a controlled basking beside a Californian swimming pool, sumptuous meals in fastidiously selected restaurants, and final farewells to the aged dowagers whose hospitality and generosity were so amply enjoyed, it is back to the stress of the classroom for another year. And nothing to look forward to for another nine months apart from a stopover in Marbella at Halloween, a short jaunt to the Canaries at Christmas, and that golfing distraction to the Algarve for Easter week. The university chaplain fits neatly into the above category except that his break usually lasts from April to November, the tan deeper, the wardrobe ...

Ah! yes, the wardrobe. Which reminds me. Another category of priest – if such an appellation is not gratuitously interpreted as offensive by my readers, pardon this literary lapse into the nineteenth century – thrown up by exhaustive research, is the young curate ill-at-ease in the traditional raiment of the clergy and ever anxious to pontificate on its limitations. The problem of course with the young is that ignorance has a distressing habit of speaking out ever-so-confidently while experience has to stand back and wait for it to catch up. And in the modern world, knowledge, taste and judgement get into us by uncharted routes. That's another problem. The young have never lived long enough to develop a sense of proportion. But I wander.

It's not that one would encourage the rather staid wardrobe of my contemporaries, the elegance of the frock coat, the embroidered stock, the starched collar. That such sartorial grace has given way to, for instance, a garment called 'a duffelcoat' – which looks as if it was sewn together by a blind tailor for a none-too-fussy fisherman – a mere shirt in various hues of black, grey or even blue, and a plastic collar, is in itself quite beyond belief. But even that very recent mode of clerical dress, which at least had the benefit of a certain standard propriety, is now giving way to the kind of individuality that we are rightly warned about in the seminary. Overcoats, unlike the practical and functional gabardine model in the celebrated McCaul's advertisement on the back cover of the *Christus Rex* magazine, are now pleated at the rear, half-bodiced at the front and pelmetted with fur around the shoulders – more appropriate to Lana Turner turning up to a film première on a bad night than a curate in a bog station. It is something of a mystery to me how the regulations, lovingly laid down for clerics in the varied statutes, seem now to be wantonly abandoned, but I have covered this elsewhere and I leave it at that.

God be with the days too when you had to be a bishop to wear a ring. Now personages of minor canonical status, not even Canons let alone bishops, bedeck themselves at will with all kinds of jewellery. Curates' cars are now likely to have teddy-bears on the back window, miniature poodles dangling from the rear-view mirrors, and not a sign of St Christopher's picture or the brown scapular, not to speak of a rosary beads. I sometimes think that what a certain species of curate really needs is not, as the modern psychological wisdom would have it, buckets of affirmation, but a surfeit of genuine discouragement.

My own Fr Derek is a case in point. He is of course at an awkward age for curates, not young enough to be gratifyingly apprehensive, not old enough to be restrained by the imminent prospect of becoming a PP – all omniscience, insight and perspicacity, a perfect solution to every possible problem, an answer to every question, and often good-looking besides.

Accordingly, he regards himself as a sartorial sophisticate and naturally an expert on taste, refinement and elegance in such matters. If however, the truth were told or could be faced, seeking his advice on such matters would be akin to asking Dr

Crippen how to look after his wife. His own besotted efforts to
vary his wardrobe have managed to give considerable scandal,
afford endless amusement and frighten every last dog he encounters on his First Friday calls.

Last summer, in the balmy days of August, as a prelude to the
great liturgy of cutting the lawn, Fr Derek bedecked himself in a
quite unbelievably gaudy pair of shorts, the kind of migraine-
inducing garment the likes of which had never been seen in
Lisnagoola, except possibly on a discreet clothesline when a
Yank was home. It was the nearest humble Lisnagoola ever
came to an international incident. Mature matrons covered their
eyes, teenage girls giggled their way up and down the road,
children gathered in droves holding each other aloft to peer over
the garden wall, the dogs howled, and the holiest of holy water-
hens made a bee-line to my door.

When I confronted him with the social outrage, he replied mysteriously that it would probably take some years before the wisdom of Gucci and Gabicci, like that of Boff and Schillebeeckx,
would percolate through to the great unwashed of Lisnagoola.
An instruction on clothes followed. He informed me that
'fashion-wise' – he has a curiously infuriating habit of append-
ing '-wise' to every second word as a form of verbal shorthand –
what seemed to the unpracticed eye as an arbitrary combination
of ill-suited garments is in fact what's known as 'a co-ordinated
ensemble.'

The emphasis is apparently on colour combination. A fleck of
say ambrosia green in a gansy picks up the pea-green socks
which highlight the sage-green scarf and so on through several
'suggestions' of viridescence. The motif is a gentle conversation,
a balanced meal between the elements of the ensemble. This is
relatively successful when a single colour is highlighted against
a dark background. But as Derek's efforts at co-ordination so
often illustrate, when several colours are introduced in an effort
to get them to converse with one another the effect is not so
much gentle conversation as a brass band in a small room, not so
much a balanced meal as a poor dinner spontaneously regurgitated.

The overall effect of such sartorial outrage for which the laity – apart from a minority of the weaker sex constitutionally incapable of mature judgement in such matters – display a conspicuous lack of enthusiasm and which I and many of my traditionally like-minded confrères find extremely undearing, is to elicit the kind of attention that can easily turn – if you'll pardon the frankness of the expression – a young man's head. It is to my mind a blatant form of exhibitionism, with many a young curate unintentionally giving an impression of a poodle lying on his back with his paws in the air waiting to be tickled.

I would most deferentially put it to their Lordships, for whose judgement in these matters I have the deepest respect, that they would consider giving precedence in their deliberations to this serious matter over other marginal issues like justice, unemployment and emigration and suchlike, and perhaps compile a list of apposite guidelines for our less experienced confrères. Indeed, if their Lordships so wished, I would be prepared to offer whatever assistance I could render in this regard ... and indeed there are no limits to which my obsequiousness would not be prepared to descend in the event of a small diocese or even a large parish ... say no more, as the man said.

But again, I wander. Now where was I? Yes, the categories. Another curious species of clerical life is the city divine, cut from a different type of cloth altogether. An example will perhaps make the point. A city confrère, a passing acquaintance of a local 'professional' couple at a Marriage Encounter weekend, arrives to baptise their first-born. This curious clerical import, embracing everything in sight except the font, is reluctantly given the freedom of the parish. His presence is a reflection, I presume, not so much on my own limited capacities as on the new convention of importing clerical celebrities to solemnise the great sacramental occasions of the new gentry. Local incumbents are now often reduced to the ganymede status of holding the platter of rings or the holy water and smiling benignly in a desperate attempt to disguise any suggestion of anything as outrageous as resentment. Itinerant friars have a disturbing capacity for raising the liturgical ante and an altogether distressing unawareness of the financial conventions of a rural parish.

In deference to the presence of my clerical friend, the customary baptismal repast of a liberal measure of Paddy for the men and a delicate measure of tonic wine for the ladies, followed by steaming cups of tea and generous ham sandwiches, is replaced by white wine and neatly shorn cucumber sandwiches with plates of nuts, crisps and dried bananas, placed at random around the split-level sittingroom or 'lounge' as Betty Lynch calls it. We peck our way through strained conversation. Fr Joe lectures us on his many and varied commitments. I nod deferentially, wondering to myself how someone so busy could drive nearly two hundred miles to baptise a child of people he hardly knows. Especially when penetrating the rural fastnesses beyond Lucan seemed such a devastating experience.

Fr Joe made no secret of his impression, shared by many of our city confrères, that their rural brethren live calm and tranquil lives, sequestered in some balmy rustic paradise. As he spoke, Lisnagoola took on the mantle of the veritable groves of Arcady, with new-born lambs dancing along the rolling breast of Slieve Gowna, carpeted by a dappled turf and spangled with coloured flowers, larks spilling silvery cascades of song, and the local pastor tending his begonias as nubile damsels prance around the headlands and salubrious young men dally at the crossroads ... and all on nuts and white wine.

Fr Joe contrasted the harshness and movement of city life with the silence and ease of the country, and in bold strokes drawing such spectacularly laughable conclusions that I began to wonder whether in fact he had a background in sociology. My worst fears were realised when he began to make statistical comparisons between Lisnagoola and his 'own patch' in suburbia. He tripped off the relevant 'info', as he called it, about population levels, personnel and so on, and, having extracted with some difficulty corresponding information about Lisnagoola, set about drawing instant and extravagent conclusions as if he were a computer specifically designed for the purpose.

In an effort to deflect what's usually called a leading question ('But what do you do all day?'), I began a long preamble about the quiet tenor of rural life and attempted to show that what

looked to the casual eye like dereliction was really part of some
long-term plan. Joe's distressing habit of raising and lowering
his eyebrows and holding his head at a quizzical tilt indicated
that he wasn't totally convinced by my arguments. The usual in-
tractable problems of parish life were, I assured him, to be found
even in Lisnagoola. Someone had come to me two years ago
with a marriage problem. The summer before last a teenage
pregnancy required some attention. And then there were the
habitual minutiae of priestly life, performing baptisms (when I
get the chance, 9 last year), officiating at marriages (sometimes
even two a year), preparing for Confirmation (every third year),
as well as preparing sermons, visiting the school, answering the
post and keeping abreast of current affairs. Not to mention the
many prestigious offices that from time immemorial have been
graced by the local pastor: Chairman of the local GAA club,
Secretary of Muintir na Tíre, Treasurer of the Gymkhana
Committee, PRO for the Flower Show, timekeeper for the Dog
Trials, and so on.

I felt quite cheered in my efforts to communicate the complex
pressures involved in being ordinary, but Joe's concluding remarks seemed to indicate that I had confirmed his conviction
that clergy in rural Ireland seemed to have a natural propensity
for turning sloth into a moral stance.

Another visitation surfaced yet another clerical species. Fr Jack
is a university chaplain and his visit was the result of a request
of mine to search out a parishioner, Brian Kelly, in First Science.
Brian's parents had insisted that their first-born stay in a hostel
run by Catholic religious until he would find his feet in a strange
new world. By November, Brian's letters seemed to indicate a
seriousness, even a piety, that was somehow untypical of the
young man we knew. By Christmas he had grown morose and
moody, spending hours in the church and apparently neglecting
his studies. He had become convinced that, unless he prayed
constantly to the founder of the religious with whom he lived,
he would fail his exams. It emerged that Brian had been 'taken
over', programmed almost, by this religious group who harried
him incessantly, upbraided him for his perceived laxity in religious matters and generally filled his innocent mind with out-

landish gibberish. It was suggested to him that he go to confession each week, fast inordinately and even the practice of flagellation was alluded to as a sort of elective subject for a spiritual honours course.

A phonecall to the chaplain's office, in something approaching desperation, had enlisted the aid of Father Jack and, through his interest and care, Brian was fixed up with alternative accommodation and was gradually exorcising the peculiar ghosts that a religious community had visited on him. Jack said he would call if he happened to be in the area, and hence his visit.

University chaplains are a strange hybrid. Keeping anarchic radicals at bay by arguing for a modicum of law, and deflecting the lunatic right by stressing the importance of individual freedom, they develop a kind of benign schizophrenia from which they suffer for a time before being rewarded with a prestigious parish. And like the Almighty, with whom on occasion they tend to confuse themselves, they present in three separate forms … the pint-man, whose patronage of the popular watering-holes expands both his influence and his waistline, the sports-fanatic bounding about athletically in tracksuit and sneakers, the intellectual guru organising esoteric liturgies for small groups.

Jack, sherry-drinker and a natty dresser, belonged to the latter category. Immaculate, if you'll allow the word, in red corduroy trousers, a cream shirt, green tie and a double-breasted navy jacket, he projected an air of studied elegance. My own depressing wardrobe of unrelieved black if anything seemed to heighten his exotic appearance, as did my natural taciturnity his voracious appetite for words. He spoke not so much in sentences or even paragraphs but whole chapters, interminable monologues about how fanatical groups can transmute the message of Jesus into a joyless puritanism, the damage to individual and family that the 'cult' approach induces, the wonder that such questionable procedures could be tolerated by Church authorities. And all the while using a vocabulary that suggested he had, in his formative years, consumed large portions of Roget's *Thesaurus* and never digested it properly. And all the while I sat transfixed both by the wholly unpredictable realisation that I agreed with every word he said and the even more improbable conclusion that we belonged to the same priesthood.

As he spoke, his gaze swept around the room examining the depressing decor as if to commit it to memory, no doubt mentally suggesting to himself how it could be improved: a pot-plant here, a bean-bag there, and so forth. Later on that evening, Jack introduced me to the delights of what he called 'Calypso Coffee', the definitive convent cocktail, a delicate blend of domesticity and hard liquor. And later still that night, as he eased himself into his battered Starlet, he was holding forth on the merits of carrot soup and chocolate mousse: truly a man for all seasons.

And, talking of categories, there's the ... But perhaps it is sufficient for the day. My instinct at this stage should be encouraged to triumph over my impulse. Singlemindedness is all very well but it has a habit of being confused with obduracy, not to speak of dementia. I know too that, by and large, it is our failures that civilise us but you can take that principle too far. Lines have to be drawn somewhere, as the bishop said to the curate.

XV   Cakes and Ale

'The liturgy and devotions of the Church are to a large extent dependent on the pastor,' Canon Thomas O'Donnell informs me, courtesy of my bedtime reading *The Priest of Today: His Ideals and His Duties.* 'He may rob them of much of their dignity and effect; or, by his reverence and zeal, he may be the chief means of interpreting and promoting them amongst the faithful.' Several decades later, the American Bishops rephrased the same truth in the adage, 'Good liturgy builds faith, bad liturgy destroys faith'. I know this because my curate, Fr Derek, repeats it with the kind of fervour reserved for pious ejaculations in the highly indulgenced past, and then goes on to elaborate on the need for a truly celebratory liturgy, an obsession born apparently out of a short holiday spent with a priest-friend in Nigeria.

Meanwhile back at the ranch, the difficult truth is that, aphorisms aside, whatever enthusiasm I can muster for introducing the very notion of celebration into the Lisnagoola liturgies has been greeted with modified rapture. The lined faces of my parishioners suddenly appeared sullen and unyielding, the kind of silence that the word 'celebration' seems invented to fill. Yet time and circumstance have somehow contrived to produce an aura of dullness and a level of sheer ordinariness that defeats the very notion of celebration. They are a reserved people, with a wisdom and dignity that comes from long-remembered years of security and stability. Here to live well is very often not to change at all. Perhaps they have little to celebrate – that family conflict, the anger of emigration, and ominous talk about increased levels of unemployment have turned the Eucharist into a focus for dull duty rather than an occasion for celebration.

Their faces tell me 'Get on with it'. The real action is somewhere else. The word 'celebration' is not part of their religious vocabulary.

And yet to mark the GAA centenary, the local club organised a day's celebration. Faces curiously incommunicative in church suddenly blossomed in more secular surroundings. An unequal contest between 'Past' and 'Present' selections gave the lithe youngsters an exaggerated sense of their football skills, while their jaded opponents, heroes of other days, were soon convinced that it's easier to talk about the glories of the past than to try and recapture them. A children's sports followed and the day's events concluded with a Mass in memory of deceased members of the club.

Unpredictably, the *gaudete* spirit of the sports field was carried into the church. A native son, sometime sporting hero, was the celebrant. They were, he told them, the best parish in the diocese, their great teams were talked about throughout the length and breadth of the country, and their seablue jersey was feared in every part of the county. His homily was a potted history of the GAA in the parish, titles won through skill and perseverance, titles lost through ill-luck or bad refereeing. His voice rose to commend the great stars of the past ('Some of whom are still with us') and whole pews expanded in pride at the unexpected compliment. And his voice fell in a hush when he remembered those who were now 'part of the great GAA club in God's kingdom'.

Even the choir, usually little more than a nominal presence, was cajoled out of its customary lethargy. It was as if some touring Welsh choir, slightly out of practice, had stopped over to lend a hundred extra voices. And even the wheezy harmonium seemed somehow to expand its limited volume as the liturgy ended with a fulsome congregational rendering of *Faith of our Fathers*.

Was it the unusual event, or the sporting dimension, or even the time of day, that produced such unabashed celebration? Or, distressingly, could it be the celebrant? Maybe it was that uncomfortable conclusion that a precocious six-year-old latched on to when she asked in school, 'Why do you look so sad at Mass, Father?' Is my tone of voice, general demeanour, homily, even facial expression, killing the very element of celebration that I am struggling to generate? Are my people preaching back to me what I am unknowingly practising? And if so, who will tell me? Of course, we cannot preach celebration any more than we can preach joy. It has to do with witnessing, with feeling, with subtle inflection, above all possibly with youth. As we grow older we lose a sense of excitement, enthusiasm, even passion. Joy is balanced with a deathly seriousness, excitement melts away. Then again is not seriousness just controlled excitement? Maybe that says something about the youngsters who seem ill-at-ease, out-of-touch with the ebb-and-flow of the Sunday liturgy? What is appropriate, reverent, acceptable to me and my peers may, for the young, define something akin to joylessness, a real failure to celebrate.

The Holy Week Ceremonies are a case in point. They present the great liturgical challenge of the year. How not to undo the symbol, to milk it of substance and meaning by fulsome explication, the abiding temptation of Holy Week. To test and taste too much so that, in Kavanagh's phrase, 'Through a chink too wide there comes in no wonder', to know that 'the depths of the earth' and 'the heights of the mountains' can never be fully translated into the common currency of Lisnagoola's air softened by a spring shower. We can do no more than approach, consider, respect the symbols of God's presence among us. This I tell them is the religious high-point of the year and their reaction is a mixture of expectation and dread, wondering what possible liturgical cartwheel I will employ to retain their attention, but with a sinking feeling, too, that the ceremonies may last beyond the specified time that tradition and the common consensus have allocated for them.

In Lisnagoola, liturgical innovations are greeted with a somewhat restrained fervour. A previous washing of the feet was something of a disaster when the apostolic twelve finished up as eight, an unbiblical spectacle of four Judases predicting better than I the social ridicule that followed. Not for them the antithetic subtleties of light and darkness or the intricate itinerary through the Old Testament to situate Christ's coming. The liturgical niceties of Holy Week are, in practice, subordinate to the more tangible symbols of kissing the cross and collecting a bottle of holy water. Lips chaffed and broken by a winter wind pout awkwardly to kiss the cross on Good Friday, young children and 'hardy annuals' in a rare shuffle to the altar. Bottles filled with the Easter water bear blessings home to family and stock, a substantial fruit that validates the simple faith of my good people of Lisnagoola.

In the out-church in Shanvahara, Fr Derek ploughs a more creative liturgical furrow, a great truth to which my attention is regularly drawn. Liturgical mime, Taizé prayer and other excesses, the appropriateness of which I often fail to appreciate, excite a bevy of almost exclusively female liturgical groupies whose vocabulary is speckled with words like 'meaningful', 'relevant', 'imaginative', 'authentic', 'original' and 'real'. The catalyst of all this angst is variously described as 'a wonderful priest', 'great with the youth', 'in touch with life' and a veritable litany of personal and liturgical sobriquets, into a discussion of which I am reluctantly but continuosly drawn. All of that and heaven too?

To give him his due though, he has established a system that survives his absence, a not inconsiderable achievement. The down side is that a series of complex expectations has been created, a dispensation which does not always endear itself to those wheeled on to the liturgical stage to replace him. Some developments are admired best from theory and from a distance. Like for instance, in the case of a visit to the West Indies to which Fr Derek is periodically drawn. Usually the allotted four weeks annual leave have to be extended to five due to Trans America's reluctance to rejig their international time-table to suit the 9 o'clock Sunday Mass in Shanvahara; and then to six due to a quite unpredictable alignment of a complex series of financial, climatic and personal factors. It is, of course, the way nowadays with curates. Inches become not yards but furlongs.

On this occasion, his anticipated return was interrupted by a series of hurricanes in the area which, as news reports indicated, involved a considerable loss of life. While the unspoken prospect of this happy news warmed my heart considerably, the temperature in the local convent, to which Fr Derek is irresistibly attached, soared to crisis-point. Masses were said, novenas were set upon, prayers were offered, the intercession of a whole bevy of saints was sought for his safe return and, inevitably, fact was made a prisoner of fiction.

A short trip to the sun, intended to toast various areas of his anatomy an unseasonal pink, suddenly assumed the dimensions of a lifelong missionary expedition into deepest Africa. As is the way of nature and of nuns, the worst possible outcome was the first to be contemplated. In an unsuccessful effort to lighten the depression, I made a few ill-advised efforts at heavy humour. Even if their worst fears were realised, I ventured, there was always me. Unfortunately, this uninviting prospect had never been contemplated until I mentioned it and if anything seemed to deepen the crisis. In the circumstances I thought it better not to share my other great fear that transporting a coffin halfway across the world would devastate the Diocesan Sick Priests' Fund. In the event, Fr Derek eventually arrived home, tanned and relaxed after a wonderful holiday. Weeks later, after the cards had all arrived, to my not inconsiderable glee, an elderly nun (to whom discretion was never the better part of anything) let it slip that Fr Derek had confided to the community that, while the hurricanes were devastating the West Indies and heaven was being stormed with their prayers, my associate was in fact visiting a well-heeled maiden aunt in Chicago. From such tiny victories, great joy can be harvested.

The point of this story, however, was that while Fr Derek missed the celebration of Palm Sunday in liturgically-correct Shan-vahera, the liturgy continued as had been planned: a long and lively procession with psalms, the recitation of the Passion narrative in dramatic form, and a number of creative *hors d'oeuvres* to whet the appetite for the fuller liturgical feast of the Triduum. 'Creative' is probably the most charitable construction that could be put on some of his more outrageous liturgical endeavours. Like the occasion when a cohort of his friends from a previous existence arrived for a baptism. In that particular incarceration

he had found it necessary to cultivate those who found themselves on the margins of the Church. To my unpracticed ear they
were so far on the margins, they seemed to be not just off the
page but at the back of the book. I suggested that what he described as 'an unusual approach' and 'an interesting attitude'
were in effect 'atheism' and 'agnosticism'. For some reason he
seemed to think that this remark was hilarious and smiled, or
rather smirked, his way through the rest of the conversation. He
suggested that I should call on Thursday evening to meet his
guests after the baptism.

It emerged that some enlightened PP had refused to baptise a
child on the inconvenient but peripheral grounds that the parents had no faith. Fr Derek dismissed this attitude as antedilu-
vian and casually commented that Geoffrey and Charlotte were
just 'working through' another stage of the great faith-journey.
Apparently Charlotte's mother had also provoked something of
a *contretemps* over the prospect of having a second unbaptised
grandchild. To paraphrase Lady Bracknell's celebrated response
to Mr Worthing, to lose one grandchild to the Church might be
regarded as a misfortune, to lose two looked suspiciously like
carelessness. Simultaneously to keep the peace, save a soul and
have a party, Derek suggested that if Lisnagoola was not too inconvenient he would oblige and do the necessary. I was delighted
not to be invited to the actual ceremony because I had developed a somewhat restrained proclivity for involving myself in
Fr Derek's liturgies. I knew that on this and on other occasions
the theology would be out of Vatican II, the pastoral approach
out of the most up-to-date American textbook, and the situation
out of control.

After the baptism, Fr Derek introduced me to his friends who
were sitting around sipping glasses of white wine and eating
tiny sandwiches. Plates of crisps were placed at strategic intervals around the room and the practice was to dip them into a
greenish mixture which Fr Derek whispered was 'yuppy' food,
but which I picked up as 'yukky'. Later on he said there would
be fricasse of chicken in a delicate lemony sauce. But in the
meantime, would I like to meet 'Granny'?

The grandmother held the child whom she told me had just been christened 'Cassandra Kylie Kate', but whom she would call 'Fifi'. Clearly Fr Derek had not averted to the regulation that the priest is directed by the rubric to take care that a name which can truly be called a Christian name be imposed at baptism. Clearly too he had cast aside the advice offered in the Catechism of the Council of Trent:

> To the person baptised is given a name, which should be taken from some one whose eminent piety and religion have given him a place in the catalogue of saints; for this similarity of name will easily serve to stimulate to the imitation of his virtues and the attainment of his holiness, and to hope and pray that he should be the model of his imitation, may also, by his advocacy, become the guardian of his safety of soul and body.

The last Fifi I had encountered was a poodle in Ballybunion, but I resisted the temptation to confide this consoling information. Indeed I had something of a scruple about the same Fifi in that, to be exact, it is the obligation of the Parish Priest to ensure that 'a truly Christian name' is imposed despite the fact that,

> inconsiderate parents, influenced by prevailing fashion … thoughtlessly select names that may be the cause of embarrassment and torture to the bearers all through life.

Which point seemed curiously lost on Derek and, even though the flicker of a smile seemed to play across his countenance, I decided to let the matter rest in the interest of what used to be called 'sacerdotal concord', not to speak of the injunction of the Fourth Council of Carthage: *Clericus verbis turpibus jocularis ab officio removendus*. Or the Maynooth Statutes, notably Number 20.

As Granny talked she whispered a commentary on the other guests: someone who had left the nuns; someone else who knew someone who was a theologian's sister; a woman who was in an irregular union and her eldest son, Alfie. She shrieked his name across the room and a lanky figure ambled towards us, peering at me expectantly with a wintry smile flickering over his face not unlike, I fondly imagined, the sand at the sealine waiting for the

tide to come in. He informed me that, even though he believed
in God, he was unhappy to give his allegiance to any particular
creed, and his criticisms of the varied mainstream churches
seemed mainly to centre on how much they deviated from the
Green Party. The key to happiness, he believed, had to do with
the effort to get the body back into vertical alignment in order to
counter physical and emotional stress. Alfie seemed, as Waugh
said of Rosetti, a mystic without a creed and, by construing the
absence of explicit disinterest as wholehearted endorsement, he
proceeded to explain a whole series of physical and mental exercises that helped to facilitate the individual Nirvana he so
clearly did not as yet enjoy. Naming the phenomenon, as Clive
James said one time, was clearly no solution to life's problems.

Alfie had perfected a conversational technique of agreeing with
the last point of my contribution and then transforming it, by
dint of relating it to some grandiose philosophical idea, into
something quite different. I continually found myself disagree-
ing with what I was saying and the whole conversation became
so enigmatic that it was difficult to decide whether it was all
very profound or utterly meaningless. I began to pick him up on
the terms he was using, asking him to explain what they meant.
But he had been through this country before. It was all, he said, a
question of linguistics. This opened up another rich vein. What
did the word 'God' mean? Did I know him personally? To this
latter I felt like interjecting, à la Woody Allen, 'Yes we go on double-
dates together'. What was a soul? Was it possible to hold a conversation if there was no real agreement on what words mean?
Did I ever read anything by Freddie Ayer?

Eventually I managed to steer the conversation back to Fifi and
her baptism and Alfie held forth on the significance of the occasion. He was, he declaimed, happy to act as sponsor. My mind
jumped several decades back to the Canon Law class in Loftus
Hall and the rubric enumerating the five conditions required for
lawful admission to act as sponsor. In terms of the Code of
Canon Law, Alfie wasn't even at the pictures.

Sometimes, I get the feeling that celebration isn't everything.

XVI   The winter of our discontent

Preaching is the winter of our discontent. Sisyphus, condemned as he was in the abyss of Tartarus to the eternal labour of pushing a stone up a hill and seeing it roll to the bottom to begin again, is our patron saint. Once more with feeling. And so to the Sunday homily. A blank page on a Saturday morning. Always a Saturday morning, despite persistent advice and edifying intention. Even on placid Lisnagoola weekdays there is sufficient to deflect from anything but a deferential nod in the direction of Sunday's homily.

Perhaps it's as well. Thoughts and words that invariably end up as religious cliché and homespun philosophy deserve short term gestation. A week's planning, research, rewriting could induce a nervous breakdown, when a finely honed dissertation is less effective than the usual off-the-cuff meanderings, the stream-of-consciousness homily. The convenient rationalisation is that you can know so much about a subject that it can become difficult to say the simple things about it.

Encouragement to this Sisyphean duty is everywhere, well almost everywhere. Not just in the gospel injunction to 'preach the good news to every creature' but in the writings of St Frances de Sales, St Alphonsus, Pius X, Cardinals Newman and Manning, the Council of Trent, the Synod of Maynooth and, last and certainly least, the Third Council of Baltimore. Even that unlikely accomplice, Norman Mailer, comes on side to describe it as 'a difficult art form'.

Advice too is everywhere. Avoid artificial earnestness: what Cardinal Newman calls working oneself 'into a pretence, nay, into a paroxysm, of earnestness'. The Council of Trent suggests that a discourse should have two qualities, namely brevity and simplicity: the first, summarised in the old cliché that there is more fire in the sermon when there is more sermon in the fire; the second no doubt alluding to the Greek root of the word 'homily' which translates roughly as 'chat'. St Charles and St Francis, if I understand them correctly, recommend 'definiteness of object.' Cardinal Gibbons warns against the *audacia intolerabilis* of marking out 'directly or indirectly any member of a congregation for reprehension.' Fr Thomas O'Donnell counsels us to 'shun doubtful narratives, historical fallacies, exaggerated statistics, discredited legends, pious fictions, ludicrous incidents, frivolous references and childish anecdotes ... all of which bring ridicule and contempt on the Catholic pulpit.' And because, as Pope Piux X reminds us,

> In matters of religion the majority must be considered ignorant ...and in consequence of this ignorance make no crime of entering into the most unjust contracts, of giving themselves up to dishonest speculations, of appropriating the property of others by enormous usury, of indulging without scruple in evil thoughts and of perpetuating various iniquities.

And the *Instructio Pastoralis Eystettensis* recommends such a distribution of sermons that the entire subject-matter of the Catechism 'may be explained to people every five years'.

Which is all very well but in Lisnagoola, among a people more preached against than preaching, the homily fits into the human condition somewhere between Gethsemane and Calvary. I preach more often than not because I have to say something rather than because I have something to say. Speaking to the same people (generally), about the same subject (more-or-less), in the same place (exactly), sixty times a year for years on end soon discloses obvious limitations of vocabulary and ideas. Familiarity of visage, voice, even posture, compels a subtle blending into the background of candles and ceremonial artifacts, turning the breaking of God's word into the liturgical equivalent of the talking clock. Familiarity breeds familiarity.

My Sunday homilies are received in something approaching silence. I am privileged to live among a charitable and placid people who accept their weekly diet of manna and disguise, for the most, part any appetite for some more exotic fare. Controlled efforts to elicit their genuine reaction to my homiletic endeavours are usually rewarded with an innocuous 'They're grand, Father', the measured accolade of the careful rustic.

On occasion, as I wade through a consideration of the Trinity for the fourteenth successive year, with the sun streaming through the stained glass windows of St Brigid's, as harrassed mothers invariably lose the unenviable task of restraining their restless offspring, I sometimes wonder why someone doesn't rise in the middle of the congregation and demand either a more congenial explication of the mysteries of faith or the favour of my silence. If on some such occasion, that most amenable of men, Mickey Cleary, my faithful collector and general factotum, were to throw the day's takings in the air, cry 'Enough is enough' and, brandishing the thurible, lead the assembled faithful into running me out of Church and parish, I could scarcely have reason to complain. But thankfully, that won't happen now. They listen Sabbath after Sabbath with no greater disapprobation than the shuffling of feet, the audible drone of conversation from the front porch, and the occasional crescendo of coughing that signals a communal warning that the accepted time-span is nearly over. The collective fervour that greets the recitation of the Creed probably owes less to a deep faith than to genuine relief that I've actually stopped talking. I am reluctant to take the example of a neighbouring confrère who controlled outbreaks of coughing during his extended homilies by suggesting that, in his opinion, coughing in church was indicative of 'bad thoughts'.

Perhaps, on reflection, Pheidippides, the original 'marathon man', would be a better model for the preacher than poor Sisyphus. I can manage well enough the sprint-points of Christmas and Easter, wedding or funeral, when the occasion gives a significant gloss to the liturgy and rescues the homily from its usual pervasive dullness. The majority of people, Alan Bennett once wrote, perform well when the spotlight is on them; it's the Sunday afternoons in life, when nobody is looking that the spirit falters. And so with preaching. It's the Sixteenth Sunday of the Year that gets me, the hard slog of the marathon, the homilist's equivalent of 'the wall'. It was no mere coincidence that Pheidippides dropped dead after his marathon encounter or that I or my confrères are often quietly wished the same fate by our exasperated 'faithful'.

An obvious difficulty is with that now ubiquitous artefact of modern life, the microphone. They come now in all shapes and sizes, with documents packed with acres of incomprehensible detail to explain their respective merits to a fraternity who only succeed in mastering the location and use of the on-off switch after some careful tutoring. The trick is to make them altar-boy proof, to minimise the number of knobs and switches whereby such liturgical terrors, in an effort to be helpful, can torpedo the whole system. The next trick is to speak only when absolutely necessary because all kinds of messages intended for recalcitrant altar boys or ineffective ushers can generate an unintentional sideshow to the liturgy. The prize for the most excruciatingly embarrassing production is at present held by an aged Canon with notoriously unreliable kidneys. On one memorable and possibly apocryphal occasion, with the radio microphone still turned on, the moment he reached the sacristy after Mass, he sped into the toilet and carried out the most personal of ablutions with the medley of customary acoustics relayed distinctly to the entire congregation.

Like television, the microphone has a way of making people appear more than slightly comic. Every peculiarity of voice, including my own idiosyncratic drone, is exaggerated to a degree where the sound defeats the thought. Efforts to appear intense, say for emphasis, turn quickly into rant. Trying to maintain eye-contact with the side-aisles often means that reception comes and goes giving a profound impression of impending schizo-phrenia. Badly placed speakers discharge a disembodied voice from celestial heights. Defective equipment emits all kinds of anti social sounds at the most inappropriate times. And even on a few occasions in St Brigid's, when our PA system began to act as a receiver, breathless disc-jockeys, courtesy of 2 FM, invaded the airwaves with their own kind of studied mania, and CB enthusiasts broke into the Lord's Prayer with even less efficacious results. Ease with the microphone is in Lisnagoola, as no doubt elsewhere, a skill, at once simple and difficult, that defeats the local pastor.

The greater difficulty is, however, with language. As preachers we often present as medieval theologians posing fanciful conundrums, even though the matter in hand might not always be of compelling interest to our listeners. The fault lies at least in part with other-worldly language, even switch-off words like 'Pharisee', 'Trinity', 'Incarnation' and so on. It's all a bit like the Battle of Clontarf. We don't really reflect on what it means though we can talk at length about it. I sometimes think that, if Wittgenstein were to pay an unscheduled visit to St Brigid's on the Feast of the Immaculate Conception, he might arrive at a third position on the nature of words, if such matters still retain his interest. The Viennese genius first held that each word meant something. Later he believed that such words meant something only in relation to each other. It would have taken Lisnagoola on the 8th of December to convince him that someone could speak endlessly without meaning anything at all.

The problem is one of translation or rather 'vulgarisation'. The Vulgate, after all, is merely the Bible in the common tongue. Theological truths have to be vulgarised to be communicated. I say this not because the vulgar is preferable but simply because it's necessary. The purists who throw their hands up in horror at such a suggestion often simply fail to see the world as it is, as distinct from what it's going to be when they have finished with it. The function of a homily is not to impress the local intellectual with a well-rounded dissertation on some theological point, but to break the word of God in some intelligible form for all God's people.

Of course 'translation' can be overdone. Rendering things wholly intelligle can, in effect, divest them of meaning. It is possible to undo the symbol, to milk it of substance, through indiscriminate explanation. But there is a sense in which truths have to be reduced to a currency that respects the language and the experience of our people. Religion has to be found among the landmarks of our own lives, to do for us what Kavanagh's poetry did for Seamus Heaney, to give permission to make it our own.

The classical music aficionado might well ecstasise at Pavorotti's rendering of *Celeste Aida* but Daniel O'Donnell has more experience of playing to an Irish audience. Einstein, as the critic Clive James points out, a profound appreciator of classical music, would introduce it to those who knew nothing about it by playing them a track or two from a Mantovani record. As homilists, we have to remember that the Church is for simple people too. God, St Teresa wrote, strolls among the pots and pans:

> Heaven in ordinarie, man well drest,
> The milky way, the bird of Paradise
> ... something understood. (George Herbert)

XVII The Melchizedek Open

There are no riches, Ecclesiasticus tells us, above the riches of health. A confrère, an emeritus member of the Diocesan Chapter, who over the course of a lifetime has kept in mind certain cardinal rules of well-being, has arrived back from his annual trip to Marbella, bronzed and in characteristically buoyant mood. He has taken to heart Lecky's counsel of,

> moderation and self-restraint in all things; an abundance of exercise, of air, and cold water; a sufficency of steady work not carried to excess; and abstinence from a few things which are manifestly injurious to health.

His visit, at the unsocial hour of 11.00 a.m., finds me halfway through my morning regimen of All-Bran and porridge, and on the second column of the death notices in the *Irish Independent*. My friend, who retired from active service (how 'inactive' can 'active' be, I often wonder) some years ago, is in distressingly good health. He has about him that heightened consciousness of physical wellbeing engendered by the well-diguised discomfort of knowing that the sands of time are inexorably thinning, and the unexpected realisation that almost everything is still in working order. It was a 'You should go / do you good / get you out of yourself' sort of conversation – the endemic fervour of those intent on inflicting their own personal truth on the rest of the human race.

While I keep my admiration within bounds, I have to admit that I sometimes envy my bronzed friend. In my wildest dreams I couldn't imagine myself sitting on a beach in broad daylight airing dimensions of my anatomy that hadn't seen the light of day for decades. 'Lovely surroundings,' he went on 'sea and sand

and sun and … ' I mused out loud that savouring the delights of
the Costa del Sol as a celibate was akin to someone on a strict
diet doing a grand tour of all the best restaurants. Predictably at
this point my friend related, for the eighty-sixth time, the old
chestnut that being on a diet didn't mean that you couldn't look
at a menu occasionally. If marriage combines the maximum of
temptation with the maximum of opportunity, what is this
annual visitation to the outer regions of a second adolescence by
this ageing cleric? The Third Way, perhaps, or even a fourth?

My friend, who has discovered since he retired the subtle though
important distinction between 'doing nothing' and 'having
nothing to do', is a prime advertisement for the clerical super-
annuated state. He is the secret envy of his counterparts who, at
an age endemically prone to self-deception, struggle to convince
themselves that saying a morning Mass is the equivalent of
labouring in the Lord's vineyard. As well as that, young thrusting curates, ever anxious to recuperate from the stresses of
parish life by taking yet another well-deserved break, cultivate a
studied friendship based on their needs and his availability.
And the 'head-waiters', senior curates awaiting the fulfillment
of life's great clerical dream, no longer visit him when he gets ill
to suss out positive signs of ill-health. Add to that the comfort of
a cosy, single-storey bungalow, the lucrative reputation of 'a
good office', the still obvious remnants of a widely-admired
singing voice and the features of a Dorian Gray.

A discussion followed on whether the appropriate age for clerical retirement should remain the biblical equivalent of old age
plus five years on top of that, or whether the secular equivalent
of sixty-five might not better serve both individual and institution. The struggle to embrace, or accept, or encourage acceptance
of retirement in a generation ordained 'to die in-harness', a not
inappropriate metaphor for some of us, has not been an altogether happy one. There is, too, the not inconsiderable need to
preserve a dimension of self-esteem and self-worth, a necessary
part of the retirement process which my young curate, the irrepressible Fr Derek, rather uncharitably calls 'the unavoidable
massaging of tired clerical egos'. In the event my confrère, a
lapsed Vicar General incidentally, and I agreed that the prospect

of going out to grass was one of the few experiences of clerical life to be unambiguously desired and embraced.

Unfortunately, not having yet reached that elusive butterfly state of an unscheduled life after breakfast, I have to content myself with the occasional outing on the golf course. This particular form of recreation now occurs so irregularly that my limited ability no longer defines the satisfaction gleaned from the activity. Having learned, over the course of a lifetime, that I am part of a golfing category where performance seems to stand in inverse proportion to practice, I have read the truth in the sand and now content myself with enjoying the fresh air and the imperceptible physical activity. Surely Shaw was right when he described golf as an enjoyable walk needlessly interrupted.

At the same time, when the diocesan honour is at stake and when a welcome break is on offer, it is difficult to submit oneself to the discomforts of reality. Sometimes fantasy is a more benign companion. Thus I ventured to offer my services to the captain of the diocesan team in the National Clergy Competition. As a founding member of what surely became the most singularly ineffective team in the history of the game, and as the recipient over the years of a great deal of albeit insincere encouragement from my canonical underlings cum golfing superiors, I felt I had something of a moral claim to selection. The captain, who spends most of his waking hours moving his arms around his torso in an effort to retain his swing, displayed remarkable control over his emotions when I conveyed the happy tidings.

The great occasion arrived. 'The Melchizedek Open' some wag called it, in deference to its predominantly senescent clientele. That unkind, if not inaccurate, remark should be tempered somewhat by the knowledge that the said individual had lost his place on the panel to a more senior colleague, a founding father of the diocesan team, who decided to make an unwelcome and, in the event, inauspicious return to the first-team duty. Hell hath no fury like a golfer scorned.

In fact, all forms of clerical life were there. The occasional Adonis cutting a considerable dash in Pringle sweater and Levi 501s, and pirouetting nervously at the top of his swing like a ballet dancer worried about whether his leotards will hold; middle-aged curates looking like aged refugees from the sixties in bell-bottoms and turtle-necked sweaters; oldtimers in their unmistakeable black trousers and civilian accessories rescued from the remains of the last jumble sale. All junkies of that peculiar sporting addiction that involves long and tedious walks in multifarious directions, pointless searches through acres of undergrowth, and the kind of interminable discussion of the proceedings that would do justice to Hamlet. To play this game, all that is required is the ability to stand up, an exceptional humility and a gullible disposition, in that persevering with the game demands some quite unsubstantiated belief, like for example that a bad back is inhibiting the emergence of a quite exceptional talent.

My partner, who for legal reasons I will grace with the pseudonym T.P., proceeded to explain at quite unnecessary length a whole series of tactics he had worked out over the course of the preceding winter. As we assembled on the first tee, he took me aside and, in a confidential voice, whispered explanations of the basic strategy using terms like 'in and out', 'course management', 'percentage golf' and so on, as I nodded uncomprehendingly. As Brendan Behan said in a different context, 'It was the least I could do'. It is one of the unresolved mysteries of this game that people with abysmal personal golfing histories can offer at considerable length any amount of unsolicited advice to their golfing companions. I have known men who have studied theology all their lives but who would never dream of claiming any particular expertise as a result, or offering even the most tentative theological opinion, but who despite their inglorious limitations at golf never hesitate to offer detailed, indeed tedious, advice to their hardpressed companions, while at the same time alluding to their quite unremarkable rounds. The golf course is absolutely the last place to cultivate that pastoral technique called 'active listening' in that it seems, like Lough Derg in Sean O'Faolain's phrase, to 'stimulate the autobiographical in people'.

T.P., who had a dizzying array of golfing artefacts to organise before he managed to put the ball on the tee, eventually drove off. By some unaccountable abberation, the ball squirted into dense undergrowth. His analysis of the drive was that he 'came up off it a bit' and the solution to his consequent predicament was to take several hacks in progressively indisciplined fury that did more to redesign one particular part of the course than to actually move the ball. After some encouragement, T.P. 'got his swing going'. The problem was that, even though he could hit the ball quite prodigious distances and the trajectory was a delight to behold, the direction left a lot to be desired. The more I encouraged him, the wilder the swing became and the wider off the mark he finished. I decided to adopt what psychologists call 'a policy of intermittent reinforcement', occasional rather than sustained affirmation.

Our opponents, who seemed more than slightly bemused at our adventures, played steady but, in T.P.'s estimation, unexciting golf. Every shot was discussed, planned, executed and analysed with deadly seriousness. Known widely as Beamish and Crawford for their patronage of the nineteenth hole, they had also a national reputation for nursing their handicaps and carrying off, to the ignominy and envy of their co-diocesans, innumerable prestigious prizes. They had, too, a disconcerting habit of giving themselves the benefit of the doubt in ambivalent situations. T.P. confided to me, as their hilarity grew at our erratic performances, that he would sooner or later put 'a halt to their gallop', 'soften their cough' sort of thing.

The inevitable altercation took place at the fourteenth hole. Crawford's ball had come to rest on a loose matt of dead vegetation on a precipitous slope. Every time he addressed it, it snuggled deeper into the vegetation, a movement which in T.P.'s opinion warranted a one stroke penalty. Beamish, on the other hand, argued that while he conceded that the ball actually moved, its lie never changed, the situation being similar to the case of a ball being lodged in the branch of a tree which is deemed not to move even though the bough sways in the breeze. A previous incarceration in a Marriage Tribunal, as a Defender of the Bond, with all those psychic anomalies in the undergrowth, had left its mark. T.P. however was equal to the task. Was the concept of a stationary ball, he enquired fatuously, invalidated by the rotation of the earth? He then told Crawford to take a four-shot penalty, adding what I thought was a quite superfluous adjective. *In arduis viget virtus.*

While my own game fulfilled my most pessimistic expectations and the diocesan squad held its place at the bottom of the table surrounded by an embarrassing plethora of 'B' and even 'C' teams, the outing was nonetheless a welcome break. Despite the ponderous strategy and the tortuous post-analysis, we performed with the usual frenzied mediocrity, but the fresh air, the luxurious accommodation and the strong drink proved ample compensation.There is, too, the distraction of a decent game of cards during which some visiting Ordinary dispenses from the twenty-ninth Maynooth statute:

> prohibemus ne quis sacerdos ludum chartarum vel alios huiusmodi ludos ultra mediam noctem protrahat neve in iis pro magna summa pecuniae certet.

The considerable camaraderie of the event, not to speak of the vast quantities of Remy Martin, consumed naturally in delicate measures, rescued the occasion from anything approaching disappointment. While the golf, more often than not, is no more than a distracting side-show, the heady cocktail of good food, strong drink and every variety of clerical company makes the Church and General Show the perfect antidote to post-Triduum blues.

The game of golf is not just, *pace* Shaw, a walk in the countryside, but, for the true afficionados, a form of advanced meditation, an inner struggle against oneself, a lifelong effort in which we build character, lose our patience and fantasise about possibilities. Like celibacy.

XVIII   The wedding of the year

On a September morning, a pleasing task, a seasonal benediction, a first anthem to autumn. Wedding invitation cards, like drunken sentries standing slightly askew on my mantelpiece for a whole summer, are ceremoniously and gratifyingly dumped. More a funeral than a marriage person, I had greeted their arrival with dismay. Obsequies rather than nuptials are my personal preference if not my liturgical forte. In my declining years I tend to resonate more instinctively with occasions of sadness, and enter a deep depression at the merest suggestion of joy. Thus, constitutionally allergic to wedding celebrations, the distinctive invitation cards, replete with embossed edges and accusatory R.S.V.P., fill me with foreboding.

Some invitations are easily parried. Church groupies, trawling the clerical depths to ensure a respectable spread of concelebrants, invite every Roman collar in the barony and beyond. A short note indicating a controlled regret successfully deflects that precursor to a day of needless despair. Of course, expressions of excessive regret will invariably occasion another invitation from the next marriageable member of the family a year hence and afford additional grounds for a form of moral blackmail. However, to extricate oneself from other unacceptable invites can be more problematic but, and I pass this advice on free-of-charge, a successful strategy is immediately to decide on that precise date as the unalterable day of the parish pilgrimage to Knock or some such semi-religious exercise. Other creative pastoral strategies are holidays, confessions, the vigil Mass (if the location is gratifyingly out of range), the curate is AWOL, the unfortunate congruence of the visit of long-lost American cousins.

With the worst will in the world, however, some invitations necessitate a positive response. A question of bearing and grinning. These are usually delivered by hand and involve a grotesquely embarrassing encounter in the parochial house with a veritable litany of standard inauthentic conversation-pieces that leave the participants emotionally drained: Isn't it a lovely card? Are ye having many? I hope ye get a good day. And so tortuously on and on.

In those curiously unmemorable decades, the 40s and 50s, weddings followed a tried and tested format. In retrospect, it could be said that there is nothing that can't be made uninteresting if it is approached with sufficient fervour, and weddings in those simpler, relaxed times were almost enjoyable. In recent decades however, weddings, through commerical, cross-cultural and other malign influences, have developed their own perverse rubrics. Moreover, engaged couples are wont to patronise a series of other weddings and on their great day invariably contrive to achieve an ill-digested hybrid of all the worst facets of their comprehensive research, topped off with whatever ceremonial inanity some half-demented curate has contrived to pull rabbit-like out of his aliturgical hat. *Ignotum per ignotus.*

The groom is usually in black, though not invariably. On one memorable occasion he was in startling white and, towards the end of the evening, bemused drunks, confusing him with the bride, were asking him to dance. The shirt is white, the bow-tie orange, the hair elaborately coiffeured, the elegance so studied that he gives a fair impression of an expensive box of Christmas chocolates and, underneath it all, sweating profusely in anticipation. The best man and a retinue of groomsmen, self-consciously extricated fom their natural habitat and looking for all the world like young whales adrift on a beach, are dressed in similarly unfamiliar fashion.

The bride is in white, regardless of the underlying matrimonial imperative and the penchant of modern youth for opening their presents before their birthdays arrive, with an entourage of maidens in glowing technicolour. A recent preference, in line with the god of fashion, is for mini-skirted bridesmaids. While one hesitates to question *in situ* the wisdom of such wear (or more accurately, non-wear) in particular in view of the anatomical impossibility of achieving a sitting position with any degree of modesty, it seems a pity not to point out the aesthetically unpleasing, not to say grotesque, spectacle that will become all too obvious when the photo-album is subsequently viewed.

A recent experience confirmed this opinion. The officiating priest, in fact a Canon, had positioned the three bridesmaids in the sanctuary. Their dresses, in red so violent that, *custos occulorum* notwithstanding, one hesitated to look in their direction, were not so much mini as miniscule and a series of crossing and uncrossing of legs at irregular intervals, that would do justice to the synchronised swimming in the Olympics, not only disorientated the assembled guests but disproved Seamus Heaney's maxim that 'eroticism is the first glimpse of the transcendent'.

Wedding liturgies are something of a lottery and have a distressing habit of coming apart at the themes. Naturally, the qualification for proclaiming the Word of God is a close blood relationship with either bride or groom, rather than anything as outrageous as the ability to read. The homily is delivered in the presence of that most supportive, affirmative and discriminating of audiences, a line-up of envious confrères. Naturally, too, in an ambitious effort to provide some startlingly new insight into an institution the preacher neither understands nor will ever experience, the said homily can descend – like a bad television programme – into a lot of rolling seas and breaking waves, sounding good and looking interesting but not really saying anything.

Sometimes wedding liturgies can deteriorate into something akin to an obstacle race. Complicated arrangements of flowers are placed around the sanctuary. Add to that the comings and goings of concelebrants and cruets, ministers and microphones, bridesmaids and bidding prayers, the connubial couple and the commitment candle and so forth, and the possibilities for disaster are arithmetically compounded. If the celebrant is 'on in years' and is none too nimble on his feet, the probability is that sooner or later the phrase 'a bull in a china-shop' will suggest itself to the assembled guests. Not a pretty sight.

In the rural work-hiatus of early August, Petey McCoy, farmer/ grocer/publican/auctioneer/undertaker, took to himself a bride. At 42, it didn't by common consent 'spoil his growth', but in the indeterminate tribunals that grace fireside and pub, he was 'doing well for himself' in marrying a teacher. It was, after a fashion, a considerable tribute because in Lisnagoola as else- where *ruri Hiberniae*, marriage usually invites a certain disap- probation, only death a measured commendation. Mary Conlon from Tireragh would provide (for Petey) the considerable con- solations of married life, and for the parish the coming of a good strain, a welcome break from the insidious intermarriage of the past.

'You'll come, Father', he said with the quiet confidence of the countryman of property, more a statement than a request. The formal invitation card with the gold etching later confirmed the details, St Michael's at noon on the 2nd, and afterwards at the Hillgrove Arms. A neighbour enquired what R.S.V.P. meant. 'Indeed it wasn't poor Petey put in the French bit. Sure he never passed the national school.' Invitation or not, the rural pecking order will be assiduously defended.

On the big day I arrive at 11.45 a.m. to find the church empty. Two youngsters on BMX cycles whiz through the white gates of the church and with almost a single motion grab their surplices from the carriers and sweep into the sacristy. A cavalcade of Lisnagoola cars edges ponderously up the avenue and their occupants spill out on the freshly-cut lawn. The bridegroom's people have arrived. Hands are shaken, backs slapped, compli- ments exchanged, remarks passed about whether the day will hold. Did Mrs Conlon leave out the Child of Prague for the night?

A female advance party has made its way into the porch and knelt on the back seat. Hands are joined in a pious and practised gesture of deep reverence. A quiet prayer is combined with a quick survey of the layout and condition of the church. No detail will escape their notice, no cobweb unseen. A careful finger is rubbed along the edge of the seat to register a dust-count. They genuflect and emerge purposefully into the daylight to assess developments and compare notes.

Just in time to see the Archdeacon's Ford Escort crawling into the church grounds. First one clerical leg emerges from the car, then the other, then in one motion the stooped figure propels himself forward, laden with vestments, leaflets, the civil register and a huge brown envelope.

The groom arrives. Immaculately dressed in a black velvet suit, white shirt with an edged motif up the centre of his chest and matching cuffs, hair elaborately coiffured, the elegance is just that little bit too studied. Supported by his best man and a ret-inue of groomsmen dressed in similarly grotesque fashion, Petey mingles dutifully, kissing maiden-aunts and shaking hands with wealthy bachelor uncles. Eventually, after much shuffling and hand-drying, he is prevailed on to take his place in the top seat of the church with his four accomplices.

By this time the bride's cousin, a Dublin priest who is to offici-ate, touches down in his turbo diesel complete with chequered seat covers and personalised number plates. In his early thirties, he sports a finely-tapered beard, a pinstripe suit, a Claddagh ring on his left index finger, and the requisite grey stock of the city divine. By their grey stocks you shall know them. Signing the delegation form for the Archdeacon, he gives a wry smile and quotes a Pauline text about 'the glorious freedom of the child-ren of God.' The Archdeacon's air of benevolent hospitality be-comes somewhat more restrained as the Dublin priest (call me 'Gerry') rejects his Roman cloth-of-gold vestments in favour of a huge, baggy Gothic chasuble that he pulls from a hold-all and nearly covers half the sacristy. It bears some indecipherable in-scription that looks vaguely like a Japanese advertisement for motor vehicles, a present apparently from some missionary nun in the Third World. The Archdeacon's offer of assistance during the ceremony elicits the clear directive that both he and I are expected to do no more than look symbolic, slightly quaint orna-ments in the background. I don my soutane and surplice, muted symbols of my ganymede status in the proceedings. The Archdeacon is resplendent in purple and lace, all dressed up and nothing particularly to do, and could easily be mistaken either for a bishop or the bride's mother. If he were to wear that ensemble to the hotel he could well replicate the experience of the Papal Nuncio in England who, similarly overdressed at a diplomatic engagement and mistaken for a buxom matron in a red dress, was approached by the inebriated Foreign Secretary, George Brown, and asked to dance!

The organist, nervous to the point of exhaustion, drops her fingers on the keyboard and unintentionally sets the whole ceremony in motion. The congregation rises, the celebrant, priests and altar-boys emerge with great solemnity from the sacristy and retreat in disarray when everyone realises that it is a false alarm. An altar-boy is summarily despatched to the front door to avoid a further *faux pas*. Eventually the bride arrives and the altarboy chases up the aisle to convey the news. We process out again and can see the bride entering and alighting from the limousine on several occasions as the photographer, a study in fussiness, strives to get the right angle.

Eventually, preceded by the photographer and followed by a video operator filming everything in sight, the bride, her father and four bridesmaids walk slowly up the aisle to the strains of that traditional pagan ditty *Here Comes the Bride*. The bride is duly handed over by a wavering father to the sweating bridegroom and eventually settled, bouquet, train and everything, in front of the altar, the final touches coming from an appropriately fidgeting bridesmaid.

I watch the proceedings with a mixture of interest and dread. The Archdeacon, wan and fidgety, has the appearance of someone waiting for a liturgical accident to occur. But his foreboding is misplaced. Despite his staccato delivery, Gerry is master of the occasion, explaining in simple words the scripture readings, communicating easily and directly in the homily, everything in fact that (as he would see it) a president of the Eucharistic Assembly should be. In the event, it was on his part a considerable achievement not to be defeated by the limitations of the occasion, or the universality of Murphy's law.

Bride and groom light a candle each and, later on, together light another candle to symbolise their 'two-in-oneness.' Petey, unfortunately, in extinguishing his taper, blows out the third candle and the symbolism is murdered through repetition. The photographer, utterly confident that the whole liturgy was organised for his benefit, intrudes endlessly, circling the action like a fighter pilot. Nothing less than a flying tackle or a well-placed kick would have tempered his outrageous interference. The children's choir, decimated – as the Archdeacon explained later – by the holiday spirit and the indiscipline engendered by the absence of the choirmistress, sang like dying dogs unmemorable and utterly inappropriate pieces like, *In a Country Churchyard stands a preacher and his people* and *The Rose*. If they had decided to sing *Boom, Bang a Bang* it wouldn't have seemed any less appropriate. Even the photographer turned up among them at one stage and gave a particularly raucous, though appropriately entitled, solo rendering of *I danced in the morning*. The kiss of peace was a kiss of peace. The celebrant kissed the bride, though not, thankfully, the groom. The Archdeacon and I, reared on a diet of making peace in your mind, made do with the usual awkward handshake.

Before the reception the priest is expected to 'circulate'. The trick is to keep one's distance without seeming aloof. This subtle pastoral skill is only achieved after a lifetime of smiling, nodding and saying 'Indeed' and 'God bless you' several million times. Ours is, of course, a ceremonial token presence and, like the multi-tiered wedding cake, we're only really noted in our absence when the 'Grace' needs to be said or to stand in for the requisite standard photograph. To preoccupy us a series of 'suitable' guests are ushered in our direcdon. This invariably leads to a series of intolerably tedious conversations with worthy individuals – usually twentieth-century Jansenists and Manichees – depressed with the state of the world, relatives of priests obsessed with the impending clerical changes, and the occasional drunk inflicting his own distinctive aura of sour boredom and suddenly anxious to confess his sins for the first time since his mother's funeral. Sometimes to jettison some bore, or to deflect from the motonony of constructing commercial or even philosophical theories about when or if the meal will eventually be served, or to counter yet another compliment about how well the liturgy was rendered ('A grand Mass, Father', I don't know if we were married right at all' or occasionally 'Lovely service, Vicar'), I am tempted to latch onto some chance remark and launch into a detailed but totally displaced declamation on the mating-habits of the carrotfly, the history of the cucumber or, in desperate circumstances, the working of the gastro-urinary tract. It is a distraction through which I can both amuse myself and remind a guest of a pressing need to be elsewhere.

Before the reception in the Hillgrove Arms, Gerry gave us a long dissertation on liberation theology, espousing all kinds of questionable theories and at the same time consuming what, to my moderate eye, seemed like vast quantities of Remy Martin. In other days, the Church would have suitably disabused him of such heresy by a short stretch on the rack, but the Archdeacon, relieved no doubt that the ceremony was over and no irreparable damage done, just nodded deferentially and paid for the brandy. It was his ambition, Gerry told us, to do missionary work 'somewhere in the Third World, preferably in Central America' and, having listened to him for some considerable time, we both agreed that it was indeed something to be encouraged unreservedly. Our relationship with this young clerical iconoclast couldn't bear the weight of too much truth.

And on to the traditional repast. 'Hell', Dostoevsky once said, is 'the agony of being unable to love.' Obviously Fyodor had never sat through the interminable speeches that are now an apparently indispensable part of the rituals of marriage. Petey's best man demonstrates an incompetence all of his own and the father of the bride – the unwilling recipient of a great deal of individual tuition in the weeks before, his face bearing a puzzled look as if he were trying to fill in the headage form – struggles to articulate the usual agenda of standard clichés ending with the traditional imperative, 'Let ye all enjoy yeerselves'. This extends to consuming vast quantities of drink and dancing, an activity with which I am not personally familiar but which younger confrères and religious sisters take to like ducks to water. In the present difficult climate, I suggest to Fr Gerry that it might be prudent to confine his dancing to those members of the oppostie sex who have qualified for the free travel, or 'auld wans' as he himself so inelegantly puts it, but he just smiles at me in a half-condescending, half-disbelieving way. The clergy make their own contribution, Gerry's witty and laced with slightly risqué jokes, the Archdeacon's more spiritual, my own ponderous to the point of incoherence. Telegrams are read out with the usual sprinkling of rude jokes about the kitchen table, the best man acting as a kind of unofficial censor in deference to the presence of the clergy.

After what seemed like most of a lifetime, the Archdeacon and I felt that it was appropriate to take our leave. As we left, full of angst and Seven Up, our intrepid imagebreaker was dancing to the strains of *Four Roads to Glenamaddy*. I felt suddenly the weight of all my years, that diminishing capacity for sheer fun that celibacy or eccentricity contrives to fashion into a distrust of passion, possibly even a denial of the sensual. What Gerry must have thought of us I can only imagine.

XIX Any old Epiphany will do

In Ireland, almost invariably, summer is a dismal season. While the human inclination is always towards murdering the moment with unrealistic hope, summer rarely fails to belie expectations. Out of a lifetime of drizzle, that definitive Irish melancholia, nurtured on inconvenience and irrigated with drink, packs itself into the deepest recesses of the national psyche. In matters meteorological as in life generally, we spend our days *à la* the First Law of the Clerical Life: hoping that it might, wondering if it will, but knowing that it won't.

Invariably too, lingering hopes of a clement autumn are defeated by the early evening rush of darkness. Light is a declining commodity and soon morning hoar-frost bears grim testimony to the arrival of winter.

For a farming community, winter is usually not a time of discontent but a semi-hibernation, a rest-hiatus, comfortable in the knowledge of crops harvested through a summer's labour and stacked securely in well-appointed haggards. But sometimes, too, empty haysheds and sodden reeks of turf are silent symbols of nature's revenge for the largesse of other years. 'This winter', it is often said, 'will tell a sorry tale.'

In a neighbouring parish, a bachelor on the brink of the pension took his life. Bales of hay had 'heated' and he was overcome with depression. The dank summer, when rain sluiced down interminably, is one answer to the disturbing perplexity of another rural suicide. There is, I'm told, a grim foreboding that government subsidy or increased headage payments will surely fail to disperse. There is often a communal need for reassurance, a demand almost for some sign that might dispel a growing wonder at God's apparently almighty indifference, a Knock writ in smaller words.

At the tail-end of an unrelievedly broken summer, and amid the rural apprehensiveness such inevitably brings, school-girls saw the Blessed Virgin in a field in neighbouring Shanvolahan. It was a dark night, a country lane, and to offset a suggestion of fear, the girls took to singing hymns. The vision, appearing against the backdrop of an angry sky, was of a lady in blue with St Bernadette kneeling at her feet, an eclectic hybrid of Lourdes and the Marian year, a mouldy oleograph rescued from the land of memory. The past, someone said, is a collection of photographs, some on constant display, others have to be rummaged for in dusty drawers.

The visionaries shared their experiences with the local PP who, engaged in the minutiae of a parish mission, evinced a restrained enthusiasm. It was one thing to have the Capuchins in the parish, but nobody was really expecting our Lady to turn up. The word spread that the visionaries would retrace their steps for nine nights and pray over the spot where the apparition took place. Crowds gathered, hymns were sung, rosaries prayed and strange sights were seen. Some saw a halo in the sky, others saw Our Lady in the moon and, presumably in deference to the Capuchins missioning to a depleted congregation, Padre Pio under a tree. Someone who knew someone who knew something about theology said it was all part of some obscure prophecy.

Word spread that someone else had a personal visitation from God and that on the 6th day of the month the world would end at 8 o'clock. That evening, the first Friday confessions were swelled beyond the usual twenty minutes to an hour and a half. That night thousands of people gathered in Cawley's field, including it was said a bus-load from Knock, the ultimate *imprimatur*. Traffic police were defeated by an avalanche of cars congesting the narrow country lanes. An ambulance, sirens blazing above the singing of Aves and the drone of the Rosary, ferried the inevitable casualties to hospital. A pole erected to hold a

loudspeaker became an instant shrine round which were draped
rosary beads and garlands of flowers. The throng shuffled in the
darkness, thousands of legs shifting to thousands of other legs,
flashing torches in different directions. People who hadn't seen
the inside of a church for years could be heard fervently praying
the Rosary. A prominent agnostic knelt in the mud, hands joined
in a gesture of pious reverence, eyes fixed steadily on the sky.
Locals who witnessed this strange sight couldn't decide
whether it was evidence of a dramatic conversion or a nervous
strain in the family. An overwrought religious pleaded with Our
Lady to put in some kind of an appearance. But nothing happened. This was later attributed to the raucous behaviour of sec-
tions of the crowd and some local anarchist letting off a flare in
the distance. An announcement was made that the visionaries
would reassemble on the feast of the Holy Name of Mary. The
crowd dispersed, rationalising disappointment into relief.

In the surrounding parishes minor visions were the order of the
day or, more usually, dusk. In neighbouring Carnfowler four
men in the process of felling a tree were encompassed by a
strange light and fled across the fields. In the dead of night, a
hard-pressed curate snug in the arms of Morpheus was called to
exorcise an evil spirit that produced a freakish chill in the air.
The curate, under the impression that he was being called to the
scene of an accident, was said to have warmed the air considerably. In the neighbouring cathedral town, at a Legion gig,
prayers were offered that the local Ordinary might see the statue
opposite his house move and 'be converted.' Instead he issued a
distressingly calming statement.

Since the initial novena of visions, an uncertain calm has descended upon what locals have dubbed 'the shrine of Our Lady
of Shanvolahan.' The cold of winter and the inevitable excesses
of Mariolatry have tempered the initial fervour. The singing of a
rather jolly *Happy birthday to you* at midnight on the 7th of
September convinced many of the solemn foolishness of the proceedings. But questions remain. Why, for example, should the
young, though profoundly sceptical, resent intensely any suggestion that the experience was some kind of aberration? Why
could so many reliable and balanced people stand for hours in a

field searching for a glimpse of the Mother of God and we can't get them to take the Station-Mass? Why would local religious, for example, bypass our weekly prayer before the Blessed Sacrament for the more esoteric liturgy of Shanvolahan?

It would be easy to dismiss it as a spiritual Woodstock, or another depressing outbreak of mischievous Mariolatry, or even, despite the injunction of Christ to the contrary, the perennial temptation towards a religion of signs and wonders. And it may well be some or all of that. Molly Preston, for instance, who in pre-Shanvolahan days I always found wonderfully unendearing, now weekly ensconces her quite unbelievable girth on my inoffensive armchair, presses another copy of *Our Lady speaks to her Priests* into my reluctant hands, and insists that I 'join her for a decade', the rosary beads flying through her fingers like a fisherman hauling in mackerel. Mary O'Hara, suffering for years from depression and a controlled form of religious mania, finds her customary conceits elevated to the level of a vision from God, and herself attending the out-patient department of a psychiatric hospital. And a litany of others having their mid-life crises in public. And of course the visionaries who, having aroused a certain perturbed reverence in their contemporaries, now have the unenviable task of coming to terms with their quasi-religious status.

Yet for all the excess, it is important to assess what Shanvolahan is saying indirectly to us. 'We forget', the novelist Patrick White once said 'because we are leading this modern life, until we are reminded.' And while theories can often be exactly wrong, I would venture to suggest that the Shanvolahans and Ballin-spittles of our time have something to do with a *cri de coeur* for the kind of experience that our erstwhile devotions afforded our people. It is a considerable cliché to say that the most basic task of the Church is to offer creative ways to communicate with the source of human life. And what Shanvolahan *et al* may be suggesting is that the anti-devotionalism of recent years may have starved people of the emotional experience of closeness to God.

The symbolism of the Roman Rite, for all its richness, is perhaps out of tune with the cultural patterns of our people, with in part-

icular that mixture of rural innocence and mysticism that
Kavanagh captured in his poetry. Symbols are too stark, chill,
Protestant even, for those reared on the warmth and intimacy of
traditional piety. Symbols too can be insipid things. And there is
the not inconsiderable point that the academic and intellectual
approach, important though it is, may impress the few but leave
the many pressing their noses against the great windowpane of
theology. The Church after all, is not a university. The Catholic
Church, as the critic Clive James once pointed out, has always
felt obliged to remind intellectual converts that their objections
to plastercast statues of Christ with a battery-operated Sacred
Heart lamps are objections to the reality of faith. And the writer
Alan Bennett once remarked that he could never be a Catholic
'because I'm such a snob.' There is a truth there that may need to
be restated.

We need to pilgrimage, to vigil, to search out in manageable
form an experience of God. The trek to Shanvolahan may be saying something about a spiritual longing that our liturgies seem
unable to fill, and we may not be over-anxious to hear it. The
young may well be just reacting to the monotony that can drain
the meaning out of life. The old may be simply visiting the country of memory and savouring an unexpected nostalgia. But how
can we explain the presence of huge numbers of young adult
men, that critical category in every survey on Irish Catholicism?
Civilisation, Yeats wrote, is hooped together by manifold illus-
ion. Yes, and religion too. Sometimes in searching for a new
Bethlehem, any old epiphany will do.

XX   There are no experts anymore

In this dislocated age, our frail and sometimes brittle lives are held together by a decreasing number of constants. Expected, like Lanty McHale's dog in *Stephen Hero*, to go a bit of the road with everyone, we are predisposed to dismiss any kind of advice or guidance as either simplistic or hostile.

If, for instance, at a wedding reception, instead of regaling the progressively inebriated guests with the kind of jokes that hover on the brink of *double entendre*, a confrère was to encourage the happy couple to pray together, his intervention would perish on a quiet chorus of 'Musha, God help him' and 'The poor man'. Or if Fr Jones were to tell Fr Smith that he was badly in need of a haircut, or that his choice of apparel was such that he appeared to sleep in his clothes, it is instinctively assumed that the said Jones is part of the anti-Smith faction. There are no experts anymore. Nobody, particularly 'Father', knows best. *Authoritas* is an ugly word.

It's all our own fault of course. The gradual slide towards anarchy, the confronting of established mores, the drift into relativism, all started, in my considered view, with criticism of the Diocesan Conference and the decline of the Parish Mission.

First, the Conference. Unease with the Diocesan Conference is the most perennial of clerical whinges. Men with genuinely thumbed breviaries – as distinct from those who prevail on their young nephews and nieces to throw them around in the hope that they might appear devoutly battered – who wouldn't recognise a bad thought if it bit them on the ear, have been known to wax fulsomely on the limitations of that most traditional of clerical gatherings but which in their view was specifically designed to make their lives a misery.

My own experience of the Diocesan Conference has been gratifyingly uneven. Handing in the Pope's Collection or the money for the Holy Places or, more distressingly, the Second Mass Stipends is not the most imaginative construction that might be put on time, but it does have its uses. The highlight of this exercise, which invariably stretches the organisational resources of the confrères – what cheque is for which collection? – is the occasional episcopal recitation of a list of defaulters.

Men, who at the merest suggestion of the drop of any kind of hat, homilise always earnestly and sometimes unctuously on the importance of respect for the Holy Father and the Holy See, will be found to have neglected to send in the Peter's Pence collection for the previous three years. Third World enthusiasts will have reneged on the Trócaire collection, even though they can hold forth at great length on how it might be spent. The Director of Pilgrimages will be informed that the bonanza for the Holy Places from his parish is still outstanding.

Another highlight of years gone by, sadly no longer enjoyed, was a carefully chosen reading from the columns of *Osservatore Romano*. When business affairs were completed and the *episcopus* of the day had relayed the usual advice about matters pastoral and personal, he would enjoin some unfortunate Simon of Cyrene to read from this august journal the Holy Father's discourse to a missonary delegation from the Congo, or some topical dissertation by someone called Ratzinger on the limitations of liberation theology.

It was endlessly enjoyable. For a start, it was impossible to read. Full of subjunctive clauses that were, rabbit-like, continually begetting one another, it was impossible to know where one sentence ended or another began, or what either meant. Nouns fought with adjectives and adverbs argued with prepositions. Canons snoozed concertedly in the front row, curates whispered discreetly at the back, and the serious-minded nodded sagely to themselves, pretending to sympathise with, even if they didn't understand, the inscrutable Romanese. The text, which presumably had gone through several translations, was well-nigh impenetrable, not unlike the clarifications with which theologians and notably canon lawyers confuse everyone. And as the unfortunate reader fought to the end of his text with blood streaming from his ego, his heroic exploits were invariably rewarded with sympathetic applause.

During one particularly memorable conference, the *episcopus* – who presumably had temporarily mislaid his copy of *Osservatore Romano* and who was determined to fill in the time in case someone would ask an awkward question and a valuable discussion might ensue – asked one of the confrères to put on a slide-show for the brethren. The technology available at the time to this photographic genius necessitated the covering of several large windows with inadequate black curtains, a complicated and particularly comic prelude to the main event, with lots of good-humoured advice about what to do with his curtains if not with his projector.

This homegrown Karsh of Ottawa had, over the years, captured on film now deceased clergy in varying stages of decrepitude, at such jolly occasions as nuns' jubilees and Confirmation dinners, and as their images flickered across the screen, the young jeered quietly to themselves at the uniform ensembles and the sometimes grotesquely posed formations, while the elderly mused aloud with phrases like 'Ah, Jack, God rest him' or 'Mick, the Lord have mercy on him'. Occasionally the image of someone still alive, or at least undead, appeared on the screen and a heart would miss a beat or two at the uninviting or even appalling prospect of starring as yet another dead confrère in a future gallery of slides.

But such distractions were unusual at Conferences. The hallowed tradition was the bishop reading out the same lists of, in the main, what not to do, the collecting of monies, the interminable readings of *Osservatore Romano*, and 'the call', an examination in some particular area of theology that invariably produced a lot of tension, little light and a constant acknowledgement of how little we actually knew.

In later years, with the coming of the latest Council and the arrival of an *episcopus* from a far country, the pattern has changed even though the complaints are as predictable as ever. In the good-bad old days the bishop sat at the top of the hall. The Chapter and other weighty personages ensconced themselves visibly in the front rows and extended the atmosphere of *gravitas* into the gathering. Behind them sat the aspiring Canons, PPs about to have greatness thrust upon them. Next came the head waiters, senior curates on the fringe of achieving life's great ambition. And then scattered in the back benches, the canonical underlings: junior curates as ever on the periphery of diocesan life. The cream, as nature ordained it, always came to the top and priesthood, like good wine, improves with age. It was the best of all possible worlds. A place for everyone and everyone in his place. *O tempora, o mores.*

That was before the revolution. Now, in line with the tenor of our times and the theology of the Church, we sit in a democratic circle. Where heretofore, when any discussion was held it was confined to the vast experience and prodigious wisdom of the front rows, and suffered an infrequent anomalous intervention from the back-benchs, now disconcertingly one opinion seems to be held in equivalent esteem to another. Even more disconcertingly, while in the past it was possible to speak at some considerable length on the great issues of the day from the security of the front benches, this traditional prerogative has been injudiciously terminated.

Something called The Three Minute Module has been introduced. It's based on the very questionable premiss that what one has to say, if one can say it at all, can be said in three minutes. And a distressing corollary is that second interventions are not permitted until everyone else has had an opportunity to make a contribution. This procedure ensures the opposite of what has been hallowed by time and tradition, that the fact of ordination is in itself insufficient reason that anyone, let alone a bishop, would actually be interested in what you have to say. And then of course there is the Xerox revolution to contend with, veritable mountains of paper going in all directions. On such hard times has such an august institution fallen. And likewise that other great constant of parish and diocesan life, the Mission.

A mission, O'Donnell says, does for the people, 'what annual re-treats accomplish for priests. Like a strong and rushing wind it purifies the atmosphere.' How times have changed! In Lisnagoola, every second year, we look forward, if that's an ac-curate description, to our parish mission. The announcement re-layed periodically to the Sunday congregation since the previ-ous Christmas, is now greeted with a controlled excitement. Missions now are curiously unmemorable. Perhaps they come round too often and lack the sense of occasion, the grand event of earlier days. The real Code of Canon Law suggested that 'Ordinaries should take care that pastors have a Mission at least every ten years'. The old boys knew best.

Parish missions, like good preaching and a respectable claret, should be dealt in controlled portions. Brilliance is by definition unsustainable. Repetition dulls even the soul. Yet, we find our-selves desperately drubbing up what often seems a spurious ex-citement. Phrases like 'occasion of grace' trip awkwardly off the tongue. Disinterested parishioners are berated with innocuous comments like 'We'll never find until the mission'. And possibly in desperation we even paint the wall around the church, the last refugee of the clerical PRO. Accommodation is booked in a local B & B, a pale and fussy substitute for the more relaxed pres-bytery surroundings of other days, with even the bottle of Paddy carefully monitored, a painful echo of, in retrospect, the considerable hospitality of other times.

O'Donnell has no doubt but that the parish mission serves an important function.

> There may be a legacy from the past, from the feeble or in-competent administration of predecessors, or they may be the result of the strong propensity of the human heart to-wards ease and self-indulgence. Charity may grow cold, schisms and enmities break out, societies become disorgan-ised, false principles gain acceptance, virtue loses its influ-ence and even the very channels of grace suffer neglect, if not defilement. For such a state of things a mission is the best if not the only remedy.

But what does a mission do? In the past, *à la* the Reds and Fr Conneely, the agenda was more clinical, the objectives more easily measured. There was a definite whiff of sulphur in the air, a Bergman-like game of chess for the souls of the just, a rounding up of the usual agnostics and come Hell, literally, or highwater, a bending of the knee to the traditional pieties. And despite the immortal comment of the PP, 'Now that the mission is over, let's all get back to normal', for the most part there were at least the tangible results, if not in the dramatic conversion of the local apostates, at least in the approbation of popular devotions and the elimination of many an illicit distillery.

Effective , yes, and at a certain price. In retrospect some might say that there was a sense that the ranting and raving were ultimately counterproductive, an accurate but awful word; that the haranguing of sin and vice by Hell-fire merchants just made the virtuous a little more unctuous and the sinner more despairing. In the noxious blend of threat and fear, hindsight has it, it was difficult to find the healing hand of the Saviour who came to call not the just but sinners. The God of accusation and reprisal often stifled the Lord of mercy and the milk of human kindness with which the tender Christ would have succoured those who walked the margins of faith. The God they preached was a grim reaper rather than a compassionate healer. But then it's always easy to judge the past from the comfort of a later wisdom. Everything used to be worse.

Style and content have changed. There is reassurance now, affirmation, as the nuns would say, of a good people living well, a pointing of a direction, a sensitising, a kind of local conscientisation, a lifting of minds and hearts to the goodness of men and the mercy of God. But no more than that. The modern parish mission is too blunt an instrument for coping with individual belief, the kind of intellectualised doubting that has even reached far-flung Lisnagoola. Nor can it accord with the alienation and apathy of the young and the feminist reservations of a progressively vocal and influential minority. That task isn't susceptible to any passing stranger. It falls to the local GP, plodding on in concern and friendship to lead the lost sheep into the fertile pastures of God's love, watered by the rains of forgiveness and healing, and to provide a texture of acceptance for the concerns of the 'marginalised'. It is something that no parish mission can do.

The fear now is not of pulpit-pounding or confession by ordeal, but a tolerance bordering on the bland that fades into the easy mould of life today. The oldstyle 'missioner', crucifix at hip, standing like a colossus, could never be accused of that. He had a 'high profile' before that peculiar phrase was even invented. He invaded an ecclesiastical patch like a huge dinosaur dominating the landscape, a Cretaceous Tyrannosaurus on a scorched-sin campaign. And despite the fact that, like the dinosaur, afterwards no one was in any doubt but that he had been here, he had nonetheless a certain predictability, a sense of what were the acceptable social and theological parameters.

In a neighbouring parish in my youth, in the rounding up of the usual recalcitrant suspects, the missioner had occasion to visit, in a pastoral capacity of course, a lady of easy virtue and ill repute, to facilitate her return to the sacraments. Neighbours, as neighbours do, kept a watching brief on developments. The first evening, there was no sign of the said lady attending the mission. The missioner returned the following day for another colloquy. Still no movement could be detected by the sentries on duty at the squinting windows. Eventually, towards the end of the week, the lady in question walked purposely to the church and joined the queue at the confessional. After a long and carefully monitored incarceration, she eventually emerged, her countenance a loud shade of crimson. She shook herself, glanced at her captive audience and exclaimed, 'That's the last time I'll eat meat of a Friday!'

Now we await the 'Reds' or 'S. Jays' or 'Hearts ' with a certain unease. Will they be progressive or reactionary, realists or ideologists, sociable or contrary? Will they be Pioneers holding a watching brief on the bottle of Paddy, or semi-alcoholic friars consuming vast quantities of Crested Ten? Will they upset the easy tenor of Lisnagoola life by creating expectations that may outlive their visit or, worse, outstretch the local pastor? Will they be 'repristinisers', trying to reproduce some perceived golden age of the past and ending up distributing leaflets for the Blue Army and driving the parish neurotics closer to the brink? Or free spirits working out their theological fantasies, giving general absolution at the drop of a hat, organising avant-garde liturgies, disturbing the equilibrium of the devout with a somewhat blasé attitude to the sacred, disturbing the equilibrium too of impressionable nubiles by their nifty dress-sense, and, worst of all, disturbing the local pastor by cornering personal gifts that could decimate his income. Still there is, too, the prospect of easy companionship, of hearing tales of eccentric confrères garnered from a life-time of parish missions, of clerical gossip and episcopal doings, and the promise of good food mellowed by the considerable delight of sharing the odd bottle of Chardonnay.

God be with the days when we used to have full churches every night – the women one week, the men the next – and when the Mission was over we looked forward to everything returning to normal and the delicious prospect of counting the collection to find out how successful it had been! Now it's all angst over a series of imponderables against the background of a world crumbling under our feet. So while a note of caution, not to say prudence, is in order due to St Alphonsus's maxim that 'one may reasonably suspect a pastor of laxity of morals who altogether neglects Missions' you can, as the old Code reminds us, have too much of a good thing. *Festina lente*.

XXI The Leavetaking

We buried Bridie Preston in the inhospitable ground of Carrowvard cemetery, the frozen clay almost resenting the willing shovels of her neighbours. The death rituals of Lisnagoola go back beyond almost folk memory and have become sharpened by time and custom. No synthetic grass here, awkwardly covering the coffin in an otherwise empty grave. The organic rituals demand that the nearest neighbours, on the prompting of the bereaved, dig the grave and later fill the clay over the coffin with a sense of privilege and due decorum. There is a finality about the proceedings that augurs an instinctive acceptance of death, rising from the filled grave and the tap-tap-tap as the back of the spade shapes the remaining mound of fresh clay while the funeral Aves are said: *Ad te suspiramus, gementes et flentes in hac lacrimarum valle.*

Bridie was, someone said, 'half a saint'. It was as complete a tribute as rural Lisnagoola would allow, with its long memory and narrow perspective on the world. But it's hardly enough. It makes no allowance for the private world that Bridie inhabited in a place where even thoughts are presumed not to be private. The established rural wisdom can sometimes be notoriously off the mark.

She looked older than her years, Bridie did. Her white hair, wrinkled face and funereal dress indicated an age far in excess of the sixty or so years she lived on God's earth. She came into the sacristy after Mass one summer Sunday and she told me that my words had made her very happy. I had spoken about baptism and, in passing, had mentioned that contrary to the perceived wisdom of the past, babies who had died without baptism were

165

not deprived of the eternal vision of God. She had, she told me, six still-born babies and they were buried in the field beside the house because the priests wouldn't allow them to be buried in consecrated ground.

Every morning she went to the window of her bedroom and looked out over the field and the hidden graves of her children and prayed that God, in his love and mercy, would 'deliver them from Limbo'. My words, confused and ill-prepared as ever, had inadvertently lightened her sorrow and indicated at least a half-answer to her prayers. *Extra ecclesia, nulla salus*: what crimes have we committed in your name?

After her death, Bridie's surviving child, a son, told me that she had had another child, a girl who died 'of the decline' at two. When Bridie died, her son had found a pair of tiny ribboned shoes at the back of her wardrobe, his little sister's shoes, silent and slightly morbid symbols of a life-time of pain and loss.

Bridie's story was a chastening experience for me and the easy presumptions I can make about the members of my small flock, victims of habit, like Bridie, who occupy their own unchanging private space in St Brigid's every Sunday morning. What other painful secret is disguised by uneventful lives and clichéd chat about the weather? How many other Bridies have stood in the early morning looking out over a field of hidden graves, holding tightly in their hands some other equivalent of tiny ribboned shoes, carrying burdens for many a long summer and many a longer winter, going to Calvary and back, and living and dying and nobody knowing the difference?

At her funeral Mass, 'saying the few words' was for once not the usual duty, scouring one's personal thesaurus for new ways of saying old things. Crucifixion, death and resurrection found ready echoes in her life and made it easier to tread the delicate line between eulogy and explication, the danger of being mawk-ishly sentimental and the anonymous safety of strict biblical ref-erence. Hers was a true homecoming, rich in religious symbol and rural myth, drawing substance from love of family and re-spect of friend. 'A good woman', a neighbour said, with the nat-

ural perspicacity of the common man. She had achieved a condition, Eliot might say, of complete simplicity when all shall be
well and

> All manner of things shall be well
> When the tongues of flame are infolded
> Into the crowned knot of fire
> And the fire and rose are one.

Beati mortui, qui in Domino moriuntur.

Hardly had we laid Bridie to rest when word came of the death
of John Murphy in a drowning accident in Australia. He was
twenty-two. Bridie's languishing death, the controlled sorrow of
her family and the relative ease of her funeral rituals contrasted
sharply with John's obsequies. Complex negotiations with for-
eign-affairs officials and the confusion over international airline
timetables meant that his wake lasted practically ten days, a
long and exhausting vigil of family and friends. There wasn't
even the limited consolation of his remains or the customary diversion of the protocol of death.

Instead, long nights of pain, agonising over the limited details
surrounding the accident, silences broken occasionally by unwanted cups of tea and eternal questions about life and death,
thrown vaguely in my confused direction. Being there was all I
could do. I felt alone and troubled, accused almost by their
silence, resisting the temptation to mouth pieties, sharing a grief
but, like a striken guide, incapable of leading them to understanding or acceptance. Their need was for some sense of direction towards 'fresh and green' pastures watered with God's
mercy and love, but perhaps what they got was no more than a
timid, circumspect presence, a sense of security, a promise of
future consolation, a validation of a wisdom deeper than my
words or human grief, like Seamus Heaney's memory in *Station
Island*:

> Something in them would be ratified
> when they saw you at the door in your black suit
> arriving like some sort of holy mascot .

For a confraternity attuned to the rituals of death, we often forget the logic of our faith as we envince a curious disapprobation, if not distaste, for any personal visitation from the grim reaper. It is as if a lifetime of becoming almost part of the drama of death has anaesthetised us to the possibility of ever playing the main part. All the measured homilies about the joy of resurrection, immortality and 'Easter people', seem peculiarly cheerless when a colleague dies. *Hodie mihi, cras tibi*. For the priest, death has a real sting. 'There is', a friend remarked 'nothing deader than a dead priest.'

Canon Jimmy was trembling on the brink of retirement when he not so much died as stopped living. In our declining years some live lives of quiet desperation, as if for their sins God has set aside human freedom and holds the *Parochus* personally responsible for the salvation of every parishioner. Others, like Jimmy, become conditioned to that peculiarly clerical torpor that is not so much sloth as accidie, the vague feeling that nothing is worth doing anymore, a condition from which only the odd bout of scruples or the visit of a bishop can induce a temporary respite.

The approach of Confirmation had induced an unprecedented outbreak of collegiality in Kildargan when, the previous Sunday, Jimmy told his curate that one should look after the liturgy while the other should organise the post-sacramental *prandium magnum*. As PP, Jimmy felt that he should take responsibility for the more crucial task and subsequently spent the week buying melons, assorted meats and exotic vegetables and, on the promptings of the curate, visiting the nearest market town to purchse two large bottles of Beaujolais. The bishop was to visit the local school on Friday and, to conserve his decreasing energy, Jimmy went to bed early on Thursday night. On Friday morning his housekeeper found him dead, *qualis vita, finis ita*. The curate arriving breathless and late, shuffled through a series of prayers, the housekeeper in tears, the two bottles of Beaujolais at the foot of the bed, silent symbols of the cruel vicissitudes of fate.

Word spreads quickly on the clerical grapevine. Nothing travels like bad news that could, when the decencies of mourning have been attended to and the Month's Mind is over, turn out to be good news for someone. Parishioners gather to file past the remains, pay their respects and have a good look around the parochial house. The children in the primary school remembering the old, old man who stood behind the bishop holding up two surreptitious fingers when no one knew how many disciples met Jesus on the road to Emmaus; the faithful remnant who shared many a lonely winter Eucharist; the right-hand men who deferred to every request, spoken and unspoken; the grateful wounded who remember the pain eased by priestly concern; the hostile now vaguely apprehensive about that great rural sin, 'crossing the priest'. Genuine expressions of loss and sadness mingle with the empty generalities about death that seek to disguise the lack of any feeling. 'Sad isn't it about the Canon', a man says, 'I wonder who we'll get?'

The clergy begin to arrive, that listless diocesan brotherhood: the stiff, gaunt frames of the retired confronted again with the distressing or consoling closeness of death, *post tot naufragia portum*; young, thrusting curates greystocked and casual, on an unexpected break from the dull routine of parish life; the 'headwaiters', those next in line for promotion, like the footballer in the number twelve shirt when the team has lost, hurry past in case some cynical wag asks whether they have their bags packed; the ambitious, anxious to negotiate nimbly the seats of power, make mental notes of the dimensions of the house and a vague inventory of its furnishings; close personal friends exchange reminiscences and regrets about a comradeship that time, circumstances and compatibility contrived to muster over a life-time. Afterwards the confrères drift into small groups, batting to and fro the vital pastoral issues of the day, whose bingo is in the ascendant, what happened at the last County Board meeting, who changed what car and for how much, how discouragingly healthy the bishop is looking. All human life is there. Everything is on the clerical agenda except death and celibacy .

The funeral Mass is concelebrated, in the circumstances the only authentic expression of priestly brotherhood. The sight of a bishop and fifty concelebrants squeezing into a sanctuary, that seems singularly designed to make communal liturgies impossible, conjures up a mixture of awe and bewilderment in the parishioners. The genius of Kildargan was never in the direction of elaborate ritual. The liturgy begins with the traditional office for the dead. A microphone emitting all kinds of anti-social noises defeats the best efforts of the MC to explain what is happening. Heads rise in wonder throughout the packed congregation as individual priests stand suddenly to intone the antiphons and just as abruptly sit again. Their colleagues, unaccustomed to reading the breviary in choir, hurtle through the psalms as if the angel of death was on their tracks, to the horror of the attendant religious who, by comparison, are inclined to practically have teabreaks between the verses.

Mass begins. The local choir, to the wheezy accompaniment of an ancient harmonium, emits a succession of sounds that though earnest could hardly be felt to pass as liturgical song. The assembled clergy, not the most accomplished of choral groups, give what support they can, restraining that ubiquitous clerical maverick who persistently scorns the arrangement of notes in the hymnal and insists *fortissimo* on his own idiosyncratic musical notation.

The liturgy trundles on in all directions. Even the stunted butt of a paschal candle flickers nervously, its dial defaced over the years in the interests of frugality, the final digit of the 199- transmuted beyond recognition. A trembling reader, missing the crucial 't', suggests by way of The Book of Wisdom that for the virtuous 'their hope was rich with immorality'. The homily falls far short of eulogy: when PPs die there are no comets seen, in Kildargan at any rate. The concelebrants assemble indiscriminately around the altar, ignoring the efforts of the MC to impose some kind of liturgical order on the proceedings. At the *Hanc igitur* and consecration, hands are extended right way up, wrong way down and sometimes not at all, confirming the curious conviction that after a rigid and exhaustive seminary training in the infinitely complicated movements associated with the rubrics, we are left with a minimum capacity for any kind of liturgical order. It is as if, after a lifetime of proposing theories about the Dark Lady in Shakespeare's sonnets, someone discovered that he couldn't spell.

At the end of Mass, Jimmy's well-thumbed breviary and frayed confessional stole are removed from the coffin for the final prayers. We process to the church grounds, wind playing havoc with Gothic chasuble and coiffured hair. A covering of synthetic grass, the modern effort to sacharine the harshness of death, is placed over the grave as we sing a final *Salve Regina*. It is a profound moment, an echo of a June morning long ago with a phalanx of albed young men prostrated in the dusky splendour of Maynooth chapel, a sense of the immutable bond that ordination brings, a feeling of kinship that goes beyond professional loyalty, a camaraderie that overcomes differences of age, theology, even culture. The vineyard labourers have laid to rest another steward of the mysteries of God, *vita perit labor non moritur*.

We have buried the dead. We have deferred in Word and Sacrament to the bond of brotherhood that ordinatian brings. We have done no more than our duty. But in truth, for most of us it was a mere duty, a social rubric. It lacked the personal human feeling that should grace a graveside. A housekeeper and a distant cousin were uneasy mourners, for Jimmy was a private man living in public a private life. Even those who ministered with him never quite penetrated the reserve that masked his humanity. Like Heaney's clerical student, he spent his days visiting neighbours, drinking tea and praising homemade bread.

His was a protective spirit 'raising the siege the world had laid against their kitchen grottos', inhabiting a world where good and evil seemed so unusually easy to distinguish. A hostage to the temper of his time, he had received, in O'Casey's phrase, neither a kiss nor a clout from life. *Ego sum resurrexio* was for another world, its joy stunted by fear and guilt. His was a life punctuated by a great fondness for God and the things of God, a curious proclivity for parish fêtes, garden fêtes, and fêtes worse than death, an undisguised antipathy for altar-boys, and a passion for saving turf. A character, people said, not knowing, as we do, that loneliness and separation so often parent eccentricity.

No doubt his true epitaph will be written in the memory of his people but, as we left Kildargan, there was that peculiar sadness associated with a priest's death. Something to do maybe with a life so dissipated on God's people that it induces not an individ-

ual response of love but a communal respect. And in the clois-
ters of love mere respect, after all, is an insipid thing ... *requiescat
in pace*.